THE TRAFFICANTES

GODFATHERS FROM TAMPA, FLORIDA

THE MAFIA, CIA AND THE JFK ASSASSINATION

By Ron Chepesiuk

Published by Strategic Media Books Inc.
782 Wofford St. Rock Hill, South Carolina 29730

strategicmediabooks@gmail.com

ISBN 10: 0-9842333-0-x

ISBN 13: 978-0-9842333-0-4

First Printing
Manufactured in the United States of America

For Magdalena
My Wife, Love, and Inspiration

WHAT THEY SAY ABOUT THE BOOK
AND THE AUTHOR

"An engaging work with all the "bells and whistles" that a crime book can muster. Ron Chepesiuk shows why he is a master of the true crime book genre."

William Hryb, Contributing Writer,
Canadian Sailings / Transportation & Trade Logistics
magazine

"Ron Chepesiuk is the master of high-octane journalism."

Bert Ruiz, Author,
The Colombian Civil War

"Ron Chepesiuk is one of the premiere true crime investigative journalists."

Jason Brooks, director of the documentary,
Kingpins (the story of Freddie Myers)

"Chepesiuk is one hell of a writer and equally great investigative journalist who leaves no stone unturned. He could be a player for any major governmental intelligence bureau."

Lou Diaz, former DEA agent and author

TABLE OF CONTENTS

"It is possible… that an individual organized crime leader or small combination of leaders might have participated in a conspiracy"

Church Committee,U.S. Senate, 1979

PROLOGUE

A **SUDDEN HUSH SWEPT** the crowd in the cavernous room with the soaring ceilings, as the elderly, well-dressed witness strolled through the wide doorway. It was November 28, 1978, and Santo Trafficante, Jr. of Tampa, Florida, was on Capitol Hill in Washington, DC, to testify about the John F. Kennedy assassination. Nattily dressed in a three- piece cashmere suit, a striped tie and wide brim hat, Trafficante had the look of a likeable grandfather, not the ruthless Mafia godfather the U.S. government knew him to be.

Three years earlier, Trafficante shocked the nation when he testified before Congress about his role in the CIA's early 1960s covert campaign to assassinate Cuban leader Fidel Castro. The U.S. Congress was outraged to learn that the CIA had hid its campaign from the Warren Commission, which investigated the assassination of President John F. Kennedy, even though one of its commissioners included CIA director Allen Dulles.

Established on November 29, 1963, six days after the assassination, the Warren Commission, heard 532 witnesses and reports from ten federal agencies. Its final report concluded that Lee Harvey Oswald was solely responsible for assassinating President Kennedy and that it could not find any hard evidence of a conspiracy. Upon the report's release, the Warren Commission sealed all of its files away from public view for 75 years (until 2039).

The American public, however, had a tough time accepting what became known as "the lone gunman" theory, and other aspects of the JFK assassination raised questions about whether important evidence had been withheld from investigators. So in April 1975, Virginia Congressman Thomas Downing, who also had doubts about the Warren Commission's conclusion, introduced a resolution calling on Congress to reopen the JFK assassination investigation.

In January 1976, the U.S. Congress created the U.S. Select Committee on Assassinations to investigate the assassinations of JFK and Dr. Martin Luther King. Coretta Scott King, the widow of civil rights leader Martin Luther King, Jr., met with the Congressional Black Caucus to tell them evidence had been found which might effect the conclusion that James Earl Ray was the lone killer of her husband.

The committee began its work in 1978. Trafficante declined to appear in the previous committee session where Jose Aleman, Jr., a Cuban exile and former Trafficante associate, had provided some explosive testimony. Aleman claimed to have had a private conversation with Trafficante in September 1962 at the Scott Byron Hotel in Miami Beach, Florida, in which Trafficante confided that he was certain President Kennedy would be assassinated. According to a 1976, Washington Post story, Trafficante was angry at the way John F. Kennedy and his brother, Robert, the U.S. Attorney General, were treating his pal, Jimmy Hoffa, the Teamsters Union boss. The Post quoted Aleman as recalling that Trafficante said: "(JFK) doesn't know that this kind of encounter is very delicate. Mark my words, this man Kennedy is in trouble, and he will get what's coming to him."

Two Federal marshals sat behind Aleman, constantly scrutinizing the room as he testified. Aleman had asked for the Marshals' protection because he feared for his life. Still the witness changed his tune and gave a different interpretation of Trafficante's comments in public than he did in private to investigators. "This man, he's no doubt not going to be re-elected, no doubt about it," Aleman quoted Trafficante as saying. What the Mafia probably meant, Aleman explained to the committee, was that Kennedy would be hit by the Republican vote in 1964—not bullets.

Committee chairman Louis Stokes led the questioning of Trafficante. The chairman asked the witness about the time he spent in Cuba, what he did after he left Cuba in 1959, his relationship with certain fellow mobsters, the many plots to kill Castro and his relationship with Jack Ruby, the killer of Lee Harvey Oswald.

Chairman Stokes: Mr. Trafficante, did you ever hear of a Jack Ruby?

Trafficante: No, sir, never remembered meeting Jack Ruby.

Stokes: Never remember meeting him?

Trafficante: No.

Stokes: Are you aware that it has been alleged that Jack Ruby visited Chicago while you were at Tresconia (a prison in Cuba)? Have you heard that?

Trafficante: There was no reason for this man to visit me. I have never seen this man before. I have never been to Dallas. I never had no (sic) contact with him. I don't know why he was going to come and visit me.

Stokes: Were you aware of any of the activities of a Jack Ruby?

Trafficante: No, sir.

Stokes: I want to ask you a question that is very important to this committee, and that is, did you have any foreknowledge of the assassination of President Kennedy?

Trafficante: Absolutely, not. No way.

Stokes: Had you known or had you ever heard the name Lee Harvey Oswald prior to the day President Kennedy was assassinated?

Trafficante: Never in my life.

Trafficante remained poised when the questioning shifted to Jose Aleman and his assertion that he had made a threat against JFK.

Trafficante told the committee: "As far as the Kennedy situation, I will tell you something now, Mr. Stokes. I am sure as I'm sitting here that all the discussion I made with Mr. Aleman, as sure as I am sitting here, I spoke to him in Spanish. No reason for me to talk to him in English because I speak Spanish fluently and he speaks Spanish… that is his language. There was no reason for me to tell him in English that Kennedy was going to get hit. I deny that I made that statement."

The committee ended its questioning of Trafficante, explaining to the witness that, under house rules, he was entitled to make a statement to help explain or clarify his testimony. "No sir, your honor," Trafficante's replied.

On July 16, 1979, nearly one year after the hearings, the committee released its report. It reached a stunning conclusion. Even though Oswald probably killed President Kennedy in Dallas, Texas, on November 23, 1963, it is "possible… that an individual organized crime leader or small combination of leaders might have participated in a conspiracy" and had "the motive, means and opportunity" to assassinate President Kennedy. The report named Trafficante and fellow mobster Carlos Marcello as "the most likely family bosses of organized crime to have participated in such a unilateral assassination plot."

Naming the Mob as a likely participant may have been a huge surprise to many Americans living outside Tampa, but the authorities knew well the extent of Trafficante, Jr.'s power and craftiness. Years of investigating the crime boss and his family had tied them to some of the seminal events of the 20th century.

1
BUILDING THE FAMILY BUSINESS

SANTO TRAFFICANTE, SR., the powerful Trafficante crime family's patriarch, was born on May 28, 1886, in Alexandria Della Rocca, Sicily. At age 16, he boarded the S.S. Lombardia and set sail for American in search of a better life. Two years later, Santo, Sr. followed like thousands of other Italian immigrants, settling near downtown Tampa in an area known as Ybor City. Today, with its vibrant nightlife and many nightclubs, Ybor City is a popular evening destination for locals and tourists. In Santo, Sr.'s youth, it was the thriving home of the local cigar industry, which was introduced to the area in the late 1880s.

At about the same time, a Cuban named Manuel "El Gallego" Suarez introduced Bolita, an illegal lottery game, to Tampa, and it became the dominant local racket. In a basic Bolita game, 100 small balls are placed in a bag and mixed thoroughly. Bets are then taken on which number will be chosen. Early in his criminal career, Santo, Sr. became heavily involved in the Bolita racket, but eventually he had his hand in bootlegging, arson for hire and narcotics trafficking.

Federal criminal records trace the Tampa Mafia's beginnings to 1914 when, with the passage of the Harrison Act, the possession of heroin and morphine became illegal in the U.S. Named after U.S. congressman Frances B. Harrison of New York, the act was one of U.S. history's most important drug laws. With its passage, anyone selling, importing, or dispensing drugs had to register with the government. Thus heroin and cocaine could now only be obtained with a doctor's prescription.

By the 1920s, Tampa had become one of the nation's major narcotics distribution centers, second only to New York City. During this period, the United States Narcotics Board described Tampa gangster Ignacio Antinori, the city's first godfather as the "major source" of illegal drugs imported into Tampa. During the same time period, Sal Lumia became the "godfather of the Bolita racket."

Law enforcement officials first became aware of the Tampa Mafia in 1928 when police in Cleveland, Ohio, raided a meeting of gangsters at the Hotel Statler. This was one of the country's first gangland conferences; representing the Tampa Mafia were Ignazio Italiano and a grocer/bar owner named Guiseppe 'Joe' Vaglica.

Trafficante, Sr. was a clever and ruthless Mafioso, one who preferred to operate in the shadows and move cautiously to place himself in a position of power. By the mid 1920s he had become a force in the Tampa Mafia. While Antonari established alliances with the Mafioso in Kansas City and St. Louis, Trafficante shrewdly cultivated a tight relationship with the powerful and up-and-coming Mafiosos in New York City, specifically, Meyer Lansky and Charles "Lucky" Luciano.

Lansky, who was called "The Little Man," with respect, of course, once bragged about the Mob being "bigger than U.S. Steel." Lansky was Jewish, but his fellow Italian-bred godfathers treated him like one of their own. Luciano, who was Lansky's closest Mob associate, reportedly once said: "I learned a long time ago that Meyer Lansky understood the Italian brain almost better than I did…. I used to tell Lansky that he may have been Jewish, but someplace he must have been wet nursed by a Sicilian mother."

Lucky Luciano, who reportedly got his nickname either because he survived a gang hit or because he had an uncanny ability to pick winners at the racetrack with remarkable accuracy, was a criminal mastermind and perhaps the most important mobster in U.S. history. As a brilliant strategist, Lucky had a hand in the criminal rackets nationwide, from New York City to Las Vegas to the West Coast. He eliminated his rivals in the so-called Castellemmarese War, which established the modern Italian American Mafia.

The Castellemmarese War, so named for the city in Sicily that sent so many mobsters to America, pitted powerful Mob bosses Salvatore Maranzano and Joe Masseria against each other in a vicious free-for-all that left more than 50 dead. Luciano allied with Maranzano and arranged for the killing of Masseria at a restaurant in Brooklyn. The victorious Marazano did not trust Lucky and planned to kill him. Luciano, however, got wind of the plan and sent four hit men dressed as cops to Maranzano's office, where, in one of Mafia history's most famous rub outs, they killed the godfather and four of his bodyguards.

When the dust from the war finally settled, Luciano and Lansky organized the national crime syndicate known as "The Commission," in effect uniting crime families nationwide. Trafficante briefly tried to move into Lucky's territory, but wisely withdrew before Lucky had to use his considerable power to put the upstart rival in his place.

Recently released government documents reveal that Santo Jr. also had a close relationship with Joe Profaci, the powerful racketeering mobster, who, ironically, was not well liked within Mafia ranks. As crime historian James Mannion explained, "He had a reputation as a cheap skate Mafioso. He charged the members of his family the equivalent of union dues." During his criminal career, Profaci had to constantly fend off hostile takeovers of his territory by his enemies within the Mafia ranks, but he did it successfully until his death by natural causes in 1962.

Trafficante's relationship with Profaci paid off in a big way. According to a confidential 1954 U.S. government memo, Tampa's Diedicue brothers (Antonio, Tom and Frank) challenged Trafficante's leadership of the local rackets. The Diedicue family had the support of Philip and Vincent Mangano of Brooklyn, New York, both of whom were powerful allies of the policy making echelon in the national crime syndicate. But through the intercession of Joe Profaci, an even more powerful godfather, Trafficante, Sr., became the boss of Tampa's major rackets. According to a report of the Treasury Department's Bureau of Narcotics, "the Trafficante organization operated with the confidence knowing that Santo Trafficante had the support and backing of the national crime family."

Trafficante, Sr. joined with Luciano and Lansky in setting up gambling operations in Cuba; he sent his son Santo, Jr. as his representative.

Born the third son of Santo, Sr. on November 15, 1914, Santo, Jr. was perfect for the job and had the skills to do it well, despite having dropped out of high school in 1930 when he was barely sixteen years old. He had served as his father's apprentice, spoke fluent Spanish and exhibited managerial talent.

The American Mob had started buying casinos in Cuba in the late 1920s, and it soon established relationships with Cuban gangsters and corrupt local officials. They also set up fencing operations for stolen goods, ran prostitution rings and established narcotics smuggling routes into the U.S

Though Lansky was the Mafia power in Cuba, he had a deep respect for young Santo, Jr. Near the end of his life, Luciano would say of Santo, Jr. that he was "a guy who always managed to keep in the background, but he is tough. In fact, he is one of the few guys in the whole country that Meyer Lansky would never tangle with."

Santo, Jr., established a solid relationship with Cuban President Fulgencio Batista. From 1931 to 1934, Batista was a high-ranking officer in the Cuban military who took part in a series of revolts to overthrow the Cuban presidency. In 1940 he resigned from the army to run for the presidency and was elected. At the end of his term in 1944, he abided by the country's constitutional provisions, stepped down as president and went into exile in the United States.

Eight years later, Batista, who had remained a behind-the-scenes force in Cuban politics, seized power in a bloodless coup, and under his rule, the Mafia influence in Cuban mushroomed. Batista's government agreed to match outside investments in Cuba dollar for dollar, as well as grant an operating license to any establishment worth more than a million dollars. Lansky and his fellow mobsters took advantage of the arrangement and built many hotels, including the Hotel National, Sevilla Biltmore and the Havana Hilton. Inside, gambling casinos flourished.

The young Santo, Jr.'s official position in Havana was that of manager of the San Souci casino, but he was far more important in the Cuba scheme of things than that title would suggest. "As his father's representative, and ultimately Meyer Lansky's, he controlled much of Havana's tourist industry and became quite close to Batista," wrote Alfred McCoy in his book, The Politics of Heroin in Southeast Asia. "It was his responsibility to receive shipments of heroin from Europe and forward them through Florida to New York."

The U.S. Treasury Department confirmed Trafficante, Jr.'s powerful status. In a September 1961 report, the department noted: "The syndicate operated the major gambling casinos in Cuba, but we believe that Santo Trafficante, Jr. was the master mind or overseer (or one of them) of all those casinos."

During the French occupation of Indochina, Corsican crime syndicates were operating in the opium trade under the protection of the French military intelligence. This criminal arrangement became part of the famous French Connection, one of the largest and most important heroin trafficking rings ever established. Founded by French criminal Jean Jehan, the French Connection operated from the 1930s to the 1970s, and at the height of its activity, it was believed to be responsible for providing an estimated 95 percent of the heroin arriving on U.S. streets.

In early 1947, August Ricorde, a prominent French Connection godfather from the Marseilles underworld, was believed to have made contact in Cuba with Santo, Jr. at a meeting with him and other American mobsters, including Frank Costello, Albert Anastasia, Lucky Luciano and Ralph Capone, Al's brother. Interestingly, after World War II, Ricorde had to flee France for Argentina because he faced a death sentence for collaborating with the Nazis.

According to author McCoy, "Cuba was one of the major conduits of Marseille heroin. The raw opium would come from Indo China through the Suez Canal, across to Mediterranean to Marseilles, or it would come from Turkey through Lebanon, then across the Mediterranean to the port of Marseille. There it was refined before being sent to the U.S. market."

When the French withdrew from Indochina in 1955, the U.S. took over France's colonial infrastructure, and it was business as usual. To further U.S. foreign policy interests, the CIA continued to work with the same people in the local heroin trade with which the French had. Trafficante and the American Mob remained involved through their Corsican contacts.

The U.S. government got wind of Trafficante's narcotics activities as early as the 1940s. A 1961 Bureau of Narcotics Treasury Department report noted that "in the 1940s, Trafficante, Sr. displayed evidence of having made large sums of money and was strongly suspected of having financed imported narcotics transactions."

During the 1940s, the Federal Bureau of Narcotics launched a joint investigation with U.S. Customs officials and New York City Police against a group of Cubans operating in the city. The Cubans were smuggling large quantities of Peruvian cocaine to the United States via Cuba. On October 8, 1953, George Zarate, one of the principal figures in the trafficking ring, met with Trafficante at the President Hotel in Cuba. According to the U.S. Treasury Department: "It was reported to us at the time that Zarate was still

engaged in narcotics traffic, acting as an interme-
diary between Peruvian sources of illicit cocaine
and American gangster customers such as Santo
Trafficante." Unlike heroin, which, upon arriving
in Cuba, was not sold locally but transported to
the U.S market, cocaine had a well-established
customer base on the island.

In 1957, the U.S. Treasury Department's
Federal Bureau of Narcotics linked Santo Trafficante, Jr. with notorious New York City mobster
Frank Scalise, who had purchased 20 kilograms
of heroin from a Corsican drug gang in Marseille.
Scalise already had a customer in New York City
from whom he could collect an advanced payment
for the heroin. But when the ship carrying the
heroin arrived at New York City port, it was not
unloaded. Instead, the ship returned to Marseille,
France, where smugglers tried to dump the load
before the ship pulled out for Barcelona, Spain.
The ship's captain, however, discovered the heroin
in the shipment and turned it over to the Spanish
authorities when the ship docked in Barcelona.

The smuggling operation had turned into a
disaster, and Scalise had to go to the customer to
explain the screw up. The customer obviously did
not believe him, for Scalise was found murdered
on a New York City street. Among the gangster's
papers, the authorities discovered the name of
Santo Trafficante, Jr. and his address --2505
Bristol Avenue, Tampa, Florida. The Bureau

concluded: "It is almost certain that Scalise was also an intimate criminal associate of Santo Trafficante, Jr.…"

On behalf of his family, Santo, Jr. attended the Havana Mafia conference of 1946, which was organized to allow Lucky Luciano to re-gain control of the American Mafia underworld. In 1936, the godfather was sentenced to thirty to fifty years in jail on a prostitution charge.

During World War II, Uncle Sam recruited Luciano in its fight against the Axis powers. At that time, Italy was under the rule of dictator Benito Mussolini, who was a strong ally of Germany and no friend of the Italian Mafia. Mussolini had clamped down hard on its members beginning in the 1920s. Luciano used his Mafia contacts in Sicily to help the U.S. with espionage, and he relied on the Mob's power and influence to keep the New York waterfront free from the threat of Nazi saboteurs during the war. As part of the deal, Luciano was pardoned and deported back to Italy when the war ended. Lucky never became an American citizen.

Luciano left Italy for the 1946 Havana conference meeting, journeying to Caracas, Venezuela, and from there to Mexico City. He then took a plane to Havana where his close friend, Meyer Lansky, met him.

At the conference, Frank Sinatra served as entertainment for the godfathers and brought a briefcase containing a substantial amount of cash for Luciano. One of the important questions on the agenda was what to do with Benjamin "Bugsy" Siegel, one of the founding fathers of the national crime syndicate. On the way up the criminal ladder, Siegel had carried out a number of killings. But as his nickname suggests, Bugsy was a loose cannon and viewed by many in the Mob as a psychopath who believed the only way to take care of Mob business, when problems arose, was with a gun. In the 1930s, Siegel was sent from New York City to California to run the Mob's West Coast bookmaking operation. Bugsy liked Hollywood's glitter and glamour, and he hung out with such celebrities as Jean Harlow, Clark Gable and Cary Grant.

In the early 1940s, Lansky, with the idea of building a plush hotel and casino, sent Siegel to Las Vegas. Siegel loved the idea. Envisioning a gambling paradise, he talked the Mob into putting up $6 million to build the Flamingo Hotel and Casino. When the complex opened, it was financial disaster. The Mob was upset with Bugsy, and at the Havana Conference, it decided he would have to pay the ultimate price.

The death sentence came down on June 20, 1947, while Bugsy was sitting in the living room of the Beverly Hills mansion of his lover, Virginia Hill. Mob assassins shot twice through the window. Bugsy did not know what hit him.

The 1946 conference turned out to be Lucky's last hurrah. The U.S. put pressure on Batista to expel him from Cuba to Italy, and his influence on the Mob faded.

Santo, Jr. continued to oversee the family's interests in Cuba while the father was solidifying his base in Tampa, helping to spawn the 'Era of Blood," which saw more than 25 Mob killings between 1930 and 1959.

Until 1950, Tampa had no true boss, and the Trafficante family operated in the same space with other powerful gangs and gangsters, including Sal Lumia, the Diedicue Family, Augustine Lazzara, Salvatore "Red' Italiano and Ignacio Anatori. Eventually, though, many of Trafficante's rivals were eliminated.

One of those was Santo, Jr.'s old rival, Ignazio Antinori, who had his hand in drug trafficking extending along the East Coast and to Chicago and the Midwest, while bootlegging whiskey from Cuba to the U.S. In 1940 he sent a shipment of drugs to Chicago, but his customers were not satisfied with the product's quality and demanded a refund. Antinori refused. On October 27, 1940, while he and some of his friends were having drinks at a Ybor City bar, a man opened fire on the gathering with a 16-gauge Browning shotgun, blowing off the right side of Antinori's face.

Jimmy Velasco, a major gangster in the Bolita racket, met his fate on December 12, 1948, when he visited a friend in Ybor City with his wife and daughter. At about 7:30 in the evening, Velasco and his family left their friend's house and climbed into his Plymouth vehicle. A man, dressed in a long black overcoat with a hat pulled down over his face, emerged from a nearby alley and shot Velasco six times. The hitman then tried to escape the ensuing fusillade through the passenger door, but fell dead in a pool of blood.

Mobster Joe Provenzano was indicted for the killing of Velasco on July 26, 1947, and the jury took fifteen minutes to convict him. At the trial, Velasco's widow named Santo Trafficante, Sr. as being one of the mobsters behind her husband's killing.

The FBI crowned James Lumia as Tampa's first true godfather, but on June 5, 1950, he was driving his 1950 Chrysler in Ybor City when a shotgun blast blew the top of his head off. A grand jury investigated, but it could not find someone responsible for Lumia's killing.

With the death of Lumia, Santo Trafficante, Sr., became the undisputed crime boss of Tampa, but he had a problem: Charles Wall, a 62-year old mobster and scion of one of Florida's most prominent families, who had been a powerful force in the Bolita racket. In 1945, Trafficante, Sr. forced Wall into a number of partnerships, effectively ending his prominent role in the local crime scene. Wall subsequently survived three attempts on his life, and to ensure his own safety, reportedly kept a kind of insurance document hidden away, a record of his criminal dealings with Trafficante.

In 1950, the U.S. Senate formed a special five-member committee to investigate organized crime's role in interstate commerce. Chaired by Estes Kefauver, a first term Democratic senator from Tennessee, the Kefauver Commission's objective was to work to pass legislation that would help impede interstate crime. As the first of many subsequent high profile Mafia probes, the Commission traveled to 14 cities, sending out subpoenas and gathering information about organized crime.

The public was mesmerized by the committee's televised sessions. Historian Carl Sifakis noted: "the hearings made the phrase, 'taking the fifth,' a part of the American vernacular, as numerous witnesses invoked the constitutional right against self-incrimination, not always in the most eloquent ways."

In December 1951, after the Kefauver Commission issued a report in which Trafficante and several other suspected gangsters were listed as being prominent in Tampa's Bolita racket, the Commission added Tampa to its list of cities to visit. The Commission subpoenaed

Trafficante and other suspected Tampa gangsters, but Charles Wall was the only one to respond. At the time, Wall was semi-retired and living in Miami, where he was still in close contact with many gangsters, including Meyer Lansky.

Wall sang for the Commission. He told about his life in gambling, beginning as a youngster working as a numbers runner, and described how he climbed to the top of Tampa's criminal underworld. As writer Scott Deitche explained in his book Cigar City Mafia, "What amazed many was that Charles Wall was allowed to testify to the Commission and yet walk out a free man—a live one at that."

Even more remarkable was the fact that the Mafia did not seek immediate revenge. In fact, Wall managed to enjoy breathing for another five years. But on the night of April 16, 1955, Wall's wife, Aubrey, returned home after visiting her sister and found her husband lying in a pool of blood. Wall's throat was slit, and he had been stabbed nine times on the left side of the face. Ironically, beside his bed was copy of Estes Kefauver's book, Crime in America. In 1960 the police were finally able to get hold of Wall's "insurance document," but it contained nothing that could harm any living gangster, including the Trafficantes. Tampa police never solved Wall's murder but suspected that Trafficante, Sr. had orchestrated the hit.

Santo Trafficante, Sr.'s reign as Tampa's godfather was short lived, for he died of stomach cancer on August 10, 1954. As he struggled with his health problems in his later years, the father had become a figurehead, leaving Santo Jr., to take over the day-to-day management of the family's growing criminal empire. Tampa braced itself for an underworld power struggle, but knowing his days were numbered, Trafficante Sr. had wisely called a meeting of the local leading mobsters, where he laid out the plans he had for his succession.

Santo, Sr., was buried in a solid brass casket with a glass lining in L'Unione Italiana Cemetery. It was a big funeral fitting for an important gangster; it cost $3,600, a substantial sum of money to pay for a funeral in the 1950s. As Deitche writes: "Although Santo, Sr. left money and property to all his sons, it was his namesake, Santo, Jr., who would inherit the most, for he was named the new boss of the Tampa Mafia."

It was a rare moment in Italian American Mafia history. A son had succeeded his father as godfather. Santo, Jr., however, would do more than just wear the mantle. He would transform the Tampa Mob into an international force and become one of the most intriguing and important Mob figures in organized crime history.

2
LIKE FATHER, LIKE SON

IF **SOMEONE HAD** met Santo Trafficante, Jr., in 1954, they most likely would have been surprised to learn that he was an up-and- coming Mafia godfather. Unassuming in manner, Trafficante was no dapper don in the style of John Gotti. Junior shunned the limelight and the usual perks of power. He wore out-of-fashion pork pie hats, off-the rack suits and owl-rimmed glasses that gave him the look of a college professor. He did not drive luxury cars and was not accompanied by an entourage or a host of bodyguards. The godfather lived like a middle class Joe, who, in true Mafia fashion, liked to hold his friends close and his enemies closer.

Later in Trafficante's life, the media would note that he never spent more than one night in an American jail. He did, however, have plenty of close calls. During the Depression, for instance, he was arrested twice for grand larceny, and, after pleading guilty to petty larceny, received three months probation and a $100 fine. The probation sentence, however, was suspended. As Prohibition was ending, Trafficante was also arrested for boot legging and fined $500.

In the 1950s, the authorities arrested him several times. A Florida Dade County Organized Crime Bureau (OCB) file on Trafficante noted that he was arrested six times between 1953 and 1958 for his gambling activities. On May 21, 1954, the Sheriff's Office in Clearwater, Florida, arrested him for bribing an undercover officer. Four months later, a court sentenced him to five years in a Florida state prison, but on January 23, 1957, the State Supreme Court reversed the decision.

Trafficante's life almost ended on January 23, 1953. As he was leaving home with his wife, a car drove up along the godfather's 1951 Mercury and someone sprayed it with buckshot pellet, nicking him in the arm. Another shot missed him and hit the rear window. Trafficante had minor wounds and his wife escaped injury. To be safe in the future, he hired a bodyguard. It would be the one and only attempt on the godfather's life.

One Federal Bureau of Narcotics document from the 1950s, which profiled the era's major heroin kingpins, called Trafficante a "powerful Mafia figure" and gave this terse description of him: "Height 5'10'; weight: 175 pounds. Visits major cities of the Eastern seaboard of the United States."

As the new Tampa crime boss, Trafficante made his first visit outside of the city in January 1955, when he journeyed to New York City to attend the wedding of Joe Profaci's daughter. At the event, Trafficante was introduced to the top mobsters from around the country. Trafficante made several other trips to strengthen his position in the Mafia hierarchy and build friendships with other mobsters, including Albert Anastasia, the era's most powerful mobster.

Nicknamed "The Mad Hatter" after the character in Alice in Wonderland, Anastasia was one of American history's most violent gangsters. Early in his criminal career, he killed one long-shoreman in a fit of rage when he was a member of the Mob controlled Longshoreman's Union. It looked as if Anastasia was heading for death row, but four key witnesses went missing and he walked. This would happen time and again. As Mob historian Carl Sifakis explained: "Dead witnesses littered Anastasia's trail."

As a loyal lieutenant of Lucky Luciano, Anastasia was part of a four-man hit squad that killed Lucky's rival, Joe Masseria, in 1931. Anastasia was also a key figure in getting Lucky Luciano released from prison in 1946 after he had helped the allied war effort.

The Mad Hatter, however, was a "loose cannon" who made Luciano and his allies nervous. As Mafia historian, James Mannion wrote: "Anastasia was more interested in killing than in making lucrative business deals." His lack of subtlety and finesse, made him a liability to the Mafia, but he was cunning and ruthless and would do anything to better his position in the Mob hierarchy. In 1951, for instance, he helped to arrange for the disappearance of his boss, Vincent Mangano, the head of the powerful Gambino crime family.

Mangano's sudden disappearance forced Anastasia to go before the Mafia's Crime Commission to defend himself. He argued that he had acted in self-defense because Mangano was trying to kill him. Fortunately for Anastasia, he had the support of Frank Costello, the then powerful leader of what is now known as the Genovese crime family. The Commission accepted Anastasia's explanation and even made him a godfather and a Commission member.

Anastasia was greedy, too, and he began to eye the lucrative casino action in Cuba. Anastasia discussed the topic with Trafficante at a meeting held on October 26, 1957, in New York City, informing the young don that he wanted in on the Cuban gambling scene as his partner.

By the time of the meeting, Cuba had become major revenue generator for the Mob. In 1952 Lansky and his Mob partners in Cuba arranged for Batista to return to Cuba and run against President Carlos Prio Soccaras, who had trounced Batista in the 1944 elections, forcing Batista's exile to Miami. Prio Socarras had been a roadblock to the Mob's big gambling plans in Cuba, but Batista had no problem with being corrupt, and after winning the election, allowed the gambling casinos to reopen.

The Batista regime implanted new operating rules that fostered corruption. An operating license would cost from $25,000 to $50,000, and a gambling casino could not operate a hotel unless it has value of least one million dollars. The Cuban Treasury Department would take about twenty percent of the collections reported, but as the Dade County OCB file noted: "Due to pay-offs to various officials, the actual amount which ended up in the (Cuban) Treasury coffers was considerably less."

The report stated that ninety percent of the games in the casinos were run legitimately, giving as the reason that "the godfathers considered the set up in Cuba as strictly temporary, knowing full well that eventually they would have to return to the U.S." But the change in Cuban leadership created a financial windfall for the Italian American Mafia. As Scott Deitche described the situation: "Havana was exploding. Casinos were popping up everywhere. Dog tracks, horse tracks, spas, bordellos and drug labs dotted the landscape, as the Mafia's dream of a criminal paradise so close to the United States slowly came true."

At the center of this transformation was Santo Trafficante, Jr., who became the most important Italian American mobster in Cuba. A U.S. government report noted: "The syndicate operated the major gambling casinos in Cuba, but we believe that Santo Trafficante was the mastermind and overseer (or one of them) of all the casinos."

Prior to 1955, the only casinos operating in Cuba were the Tropicana and Sans Souci. Both clubs served meals and drinks, which just about covered the operating costs. Gambling revenues amounted to about $5,000 daily after "deductions", according to a Dade County OCB report.

By the mid 1950s, Trafficante was part owner with Meyer Lansky in the Tropicana Casino, and he had purchased the Sans Souci Casino from Sam and Kelly Mannarino, two Mafia bosses from Pittsburgh. Trafficante also owned interests in the Capri, Commodore, Deauville and Sevilla Biltmore hotels and was rumored to have an interest in the Havana Hilton Casino, but according to the OCB, "This was not verified."

Trafficante also participated in organizing a Cuban commercial enterprise called the International Amusements Corporation. The mobster served as an agent of the corporation, and it was his job to hire entertainers and people employed in shows produced in the various casinos. Interestingly, legendary movie actor George Raft served as an official greeter at the San Souci.

Under the Batista regime, Cuba became a popular tourist destination where visitors could get practically anything they wanted. Trafficante once boasted; "You want opera. They have opera. You want baseball. They have baseball. You want ballroom dancing, they have ballroom dancing. And if you want live sex shows, they have live sex shows."

The drug business also flourished with official connivance. Cocaine had a well-established user base in Cuba because of the visitors, prostitutes and others closely associated with the tourist economy, while the country became a conduit for heroin smuggling to the U.S. On February 21, 1951, an informant came to the Florida's OCB's Miami office and revealed that Trafficante and associates were engaged in the smuggling of cocaine from Cuba to the U.S.

Given the money to be made in Cuba, it was understandable that the powerful Anastasia wanted a cut of the casino action. Trafficante would later tell authorities that he had attended the dinner in New York City in October 26, 1957, to talk not with Anastasia but with Robert "Chili" Mendoza, a mobster who worked with Trafficante in some of the casinos. Later,

Trafficante also claimed that he simply talked with Anastasia that evening about him being a potential partner in a deal involving the purchase of the Hilton Hotel.

The day after the meeting, Anastasia went to the Park Sheraton hotel barbershop for a haircut. He chatted with Arthur Grasso, the barber, as he had his hair clipped. Two men walked into the barbershop and up to Anastasia, one of them pulled out a 38-caliber pistol and shot Anastasia in the back of the head. The assassin fired two more shots. One hit Anastasia in the left hand; the other penetrated his lung, kidney and spleen. The second hit man pulled out a 32-caliber pistol and shot Anastasia in his hip. He then fired another round, grazing the back of Anastasia' neck.

Anastasia fell forward, crashing to the floor. Jean Wineberger, the manicurist, watched the hit in horror. Later, she gave this description of the killers:

"Shooter One—white male, 40 years old, 5'10" to 5'11", on the slim side, 175-180 lbs, blackish hair with a pompadour, fair complexion, no hat, wore glasses, right handed. Shooter two: white male, 45 years old, 5'7", sturdy build, medium complexion, may have been Italian or Jewish."

The killers fled the scene, and despite the eyewitnesses, no one was ever charged with the hit. It was widely believed that Carlos Gambino was responsible, since he took over the crime family.

At the time, Trafficante was staying at the Sheraton under the assumed name of B. Hall. One hour after the hit, he checked out of the hotel and flew back to Tampa and then on to Havana. Trafficante had arrived in Cuba on a tourist visa on December 20, 1955, but on March 12, 1957, requested that Cuban immigration authorities change his status from tourist to resident. That finally happened three days before Anastasia's murder.

On November 14, 1957, a little more than two weeks after what was one of history's most famous Mob assassinations, a group of sixty immaculately groomed, well dressed men in their fifties, showed up at a hotel in Apalachin, New York, a small village in upstate New York, about 200 miles northeast of Manhattan. The visitors were meeting at the home of a shadowy mobster named Joseph Barbara.

Police knew that Barbara was a Sicilian who emigrated to the U.S. in 1905 and became a citizen in 1927. Barbara did well for himself as president of the Canada Dry bottling company in Endicott, New York, but police intelligence had picked up information about his other activities. He was a gangster who bootlegged liquor during Prohibition and had a 1944 conviction for processing 300,000 pounds of illegal sugar.

The authorities had Barbara under surveillance for some time, and they got suspicious when he booked most of the hotel rooms in the small town. At the time, police did not know that the rooms had been booked for the godfathers of the five major Italian American Mafia families and most of the smaller Mob families, who had come from Los Angeles, Dallas, Chicago, Kansas and as far away as Cuba and Italy. Attendees included such Mafia luminaries as Santo Trafficante, Carlo Marcello, Sam Giancana, Carlos Gambino and Joe Profaci. The Apalachin Conference was one of the summits the Mob held about every five years to discuss business, settle differences and disputes and plan for the future.

The Mob's best laid plans changed when New York State Police officer Sergeant Edgar Crosswell, his partner and two agents from the Treasury Department's Bureau of Alcohol, Tobacco and Firearms (ATF) pulled up to Barbara's house. The officers had no warrant or even probable cause to enter the house, so they decided to drive to the edge of Barbara's stone mansion, take down the license plates of the cars, and wait to see what would happen. It was a good move, but from inside the house, Mrs. Barbara spotted them and reportedly shouted: "There's the state troopers!"

The godfathers panicked and pandemonium broke out inside the house. The stunned officers gaped as some of Barbara's guests dashed out the back door and climbed out of windows, crawling through the bushes and thorns and scurrying about like rats looking for a way to escape. The authorities managed to detain and question 58 of Barbara's guests, including a Luis Santos from Tampa. Fifty of the detainees had arrest records and eighteen had been involved in murder investigations.

Speculation abounded about the agenda of the Apalachin conference. One theory put forth held that the meeting was a forum for the crowning of Carlos Gambino as the "Godfather of Godfathers." But other sources noted key absentees at the meeting—Lucky Luciano, Meyer Lansky and Frank Costello, all Genovese rivals—and concluded there could have been a conspiracy to set up Genovese by making the police aware of the meeting.

On December 23, 1957, Corporal Vincent Vasisko of the New York State Police informed the FBI that he had interviewed a man claiming to be Luis Santos. The trooper said the person had no identification on him and no labels stitched into his clothing, but he did have an envelope containing an airline ticket to Newark, New Jersey. The name Mr. Klein appeared on the envelope, but after viewing a photograph of Santo Trafficante, Jr., which the Tampa, Florida police department made available, the trooper recognized the photo as being that of the man who called himself Luis Santos.

Later, New York State Police trooper Frederick Allen Tiffany explained that on the afternoon of November 14, 1957, he had picked up an individual in the backwoods of Barbara's residence. Tiffany also positively identified a photo of Santo, Jr., taken by the Tampa Police department and as being identical with the individual claiming to be Lois Santos.

In Cuba, Jorge Pena Herrera, an official with the Cuban National Police interviewed Trafficante in January 1958. Herrera informed the FBI that Trafficante admitted being a close personal friend of Anastasia, that he had contacted Anastasia on many occasions while visiting New York City and that, yes, indeed, he had been with Anastasia in his hotel room the night before his murder. Trafficante, however, denied having anything to do with it. "I was in New York for business reasons to meet Chili Mendoza," the godfather told the Cuban authorities.

Meanwhile back in the U.S., the Apalachin meeting turned out to be a major blunder for the Mafia and a major turning point in U.S. organized crime history. For three decades, FBI Director J. Edgar Hoover had been denying the existence of anything called the Mafia or organized crime. As Sifakis explained: "It was a convenient stance for Hoover; after all, you could hardly be compelled to combat what did not exist."

But the Apalachin raid forced the FBI to reassess its position on organized crime. In his autobiography, The Bureau: My Thirty Years in Hoover's FBI, William C. Sullivan, a Hoover assistant, described what happened. "Hoover knew he could no longer duck and dodge and weave his way out of confrontation with the Mafia, and he realized that his policy of non recognition left him and the FBI open to criticism."

In November 1957, grand jury subpoenas were issued for Trafficante and the other gangsters who had attended the Apalachin meeting. It was not until May 17, 1959, that a New York City grand jury indicted twenty-seven of the Apalachin attendees for conspiring to obstruct justice. Santo Trafficante was named a co-conspirator but not a defendant. On December 18, 1959, a jury found the attendees guilty, and the following month, a U.S. District Court sentenced the defendants. But on November 18, 1960, an Appeals Court reversed the convictions.

The Apalachin meeting did not turn out to be crowning moment for Genovese. Within a year, the godfather and a number of his associates

were convicted in a narcotics conspiracy, the
result of a set up by his enemies within the Mob.
Genovese was sent to prison in 1959 for 15 years
and died there in 1969.

Meanwhile, back in Cuba, the times were
changing. A young revolutionary named Fidel
Castro was trying to overthrow the corrupt regime of Fulgencio Batista and transform Cuba
into the first communist state in the western
hemisphere. On July 26, 1953, he prepared to
mount an attack on Batista's largest military garrison, the Moncada Barracks, which was located
outside Santiago de Cuba. A routine military
patrol, however, discovered Castro and his men
while they were sleeping and arrested them. He
was sentenced to fifteen years, but was released
in May 1955 and granted a general amnesty by
Batista. Castro went into exile in Mexico, but he
did not give up his revolutionary dream.

Castro founded the July 26 Movement, and
on December 2, 1956, he and a guerrilla force
of 83 men landed in Cuba. Only some eleven
to twenty of Castro's men survived, and they
retreated to the Sierra Maestra Mountains in
the eastern part of the island. From there, Castro
began a counter attack against the Batista regime
that changed history.

The support for Castro steadily grew. The
Batista regime had murdered more than 20,000
people and injured and jailed thousands more,

and Castro's campaign captured the imagination of the Cuban people. The revolutionary movement was gaining in strength, but the Italian American Mafia remained confident that nothing would change in Cuba if Castro came to power. As Deitche explained, "Most mobsters seemed oblivious to the dangers (of Castro). They reasoned that if they could bribe Batista so easily, then there would be no problem with Castro." Trafficante and his associates would be in for a rude awakening.

3
KILL THE BEARD

TRAFFICANTE SAW THAT Castro's revolutionary movement was gaining momentum, so he wisely hedged his bets and did not cast his lot completely with the corrupt Batista regime. In the early 1990s, Frank Ragano, Trafficante's long-time lawyer, revealed that Trafficante told him in 1958 that Trafficante and his friends were secretly contributing to the Castro rebels, as well as to Batista. "Santo figured that no matter who won the war, he would emerge safe and sound," Ragano recalled. "All the bets were covered."

It was wishful thinking; Trafficante bet wrong. In reality, Castro closed down the vice center of the Caribbean on New Year's Day, 1959, when he marched triumphantly into Havana and proclaimed victory. "I'm going to run all those fascist mobsters, all those American gangsters out of Cuba," Castro declared.

Batista plundered the state treasury and loaded three cargo planes with booty before flying into exile to Florida via the Dominican Republic. Lansky joined Batista on one of the last flights out of Cuba, later lamenting that he had to leave $17 million in cold cash behind before he had a chance to transfer the money to a Swiss bank.

Castro not only closed down the casinos, he also emptied their safes and interned the mobsters who were slow to flee. Trafficante managed to send a large amount of his casino profits--about half a million dollars-- to Tampa. The godfather also reportedly set up a Swiss bank account under the Sans Souci Casino name into which he deposited $8 million. But the report's accuracy is questionable, given the evidence that he faced financial difficulties after returning to the U.S.

Trafficante could not take care of all his Cuban affairs in time. In June 1960, Castro had him arrested and locked up in Tiscornia Prison. Trafficante managed to live quite well as a prisoner. He is believed to have used American dollars to pay off the guards and perhaps even Castro himself so that people could visit and bring him specially cooked food.

The FBI files that the Bureau kept on Trafficante includes excerpts of a July 1959 La Gaceta magazine interview with Trafficante, conducted by the publication's editor, Roland Manteiga. The editor reported finding Trafficante in "the pink of health," and wrote that Trafficante's "lovely and gentle wife spend many hours of the day with him in the garden of Tiscornia."

Trafficante was allowed a radio and TV, another inmate revealed, and he watched all of Castro's televised public appearances. Castro even allowed Trafficante to leave one day so Trafficante could attend his daughter's wedding in Havana. Trafficante said he was an admirer of Castro.

The godfather's enemies in the U.S. saw his imprisonment as a golden opportunity to get rid of him. A team of four assassins was dispatched to kill Trafficante, but Castro's agents captured them. Curiously, rather than imprison the hit men, Castro sent them back to the U.S. with a stern warning: don't try such a thing again on Cuban soil. Castro actually planned to execute Trafficante who grew desperate and called Ragano in Florida, urging him to do something about his dire situation.

Somehow, Trafficante managed to get a stay of execution and was deported to the U.S. Many questions still remain about Trafficante's time in Cuban prison and how he got out. Did Trafficante bribe Castro? Did his Mafia friends intercede with Castro on his behalf? Later, rumors circulated in Miami's exile community about how Trafficante had, in fact, established a close relationship with Castro and could even have been a spy for him. The continuing mystery surrounding Trafficante's last days in Cuba has helped make him one of the most enigmatic figures in Mafia history.

One of those mysteries relates to the most famous assassination in modern American history. On November 26, 1963, two days after Jack Ruby gunned down Lee Harvey, the alleged assassin of President John F. Kennedy, a British journalist named John Wilson-Hudson walked into an American Embassy in London with some explosive information.

According to declassified cables, Wilson-Hudson gave information to the American Embassy in London, indicating that an "American gangster type" named Ruby was in Cuba around 1959 and may have had something to do with Trafficante's prison release. He claimed that Ruby came to see Trafficante with the person who brought the godfather his special food. It is known for certain that Wilson himself was working in Cuba at the time of Ruby's alleged visit, and he was jailed by Castro before being deported.

Born in Chicago in 1911, Ruby was a small-time hood who had well-established contacts in the Dallas and Chicago underworlds. It is believed Ruby ran guns to Cuba during the revolution, with the smuggling overseen by a Norman "Roughhouse" Rothman, an under boss of a Pennsylvania Mob family and a Trafficante associate. A common link to Ruby and Rothman was Lewis McWillie, the pit boss at a Trafficante property in Cuba, the Capri Hotel. McWillie had operated a number of nightclubs in Dallas and became Ruby's friend. Like Rothman and Ruby, McWillie ran guns for the anti-Castro movement during the late 1950s.

McWillie confirmed what Wilson-Hudson had told the American Embassy. Ruby had traveled to Cuba in 1959. Ruby's presence in Cuba was also confirmed by postcards he sent back to the dancers at the Carousel Club, a nightclub he owned in Dallas, and by Gary Hemming, a CIA agent, who said he saw Ruby in 1959 at a meeting focused on efforts to release Trafficante from jail. Some sources claim that Ruby was working as a middleman in Cuba, and, that, acting on orders from McWillie, Ruby was trying to buy Trafficante's freedom by selling black market Jeeps to Castro.

Whatever the true story, Trafficante was back in the U.S., establishing a base in South Florida and making contact with leaders of the growing Cuban exile community plotting to over throw Castro. Trafficante had taken a financial bath in Cuba, and money must have been an issue for him. Government records show that in 1961 he sold his house on Bristol Street in Tampa to a Vicente Amato, then leased the property back for

$200 a month. A FBI special agent questioned Amato on March 9, 1961. In his opinion, Amato told the agent, Trafficante was broke. Trafficante later bought the house back and sold it.

In the same year, the U.S. Treasury Department's Federal Bureau of Narcotics issued a report that indicated Castro may have had something to do with Trafficante's financial situation. On July 21, federal narcotics agent Eugene Marshall reported to the Bureau that Castro had ordered his operatives in Tampa and Miami to make heavy Bolita bets with Santo Trafficante's organization. The operatives, according to federal narcotics agent Marshall, took note of which numbers got the heaviest play in the Miami and Tampa areas and then played the numbers themselves.

Prior to the Bolita drawing each Saturday, these operatives communicated with their leaders in Cuba and advised them which numbers received the heaviest play. The Cuba lottery officials then rigged the drawing in such way as to make certain those numbers appeared, thereby forcing Trafficante's Bolita players to win.

The report cautioned that the information could not be verified, but added: "if this is true, there is a possibility that Trafficante, Jr. will again be active in the illicit narcotics trade." Agent Marshall's source for the alleged Castro plot against Trafficante told him that, for some unknown reason, Castro hates Trafficante.

While Trafficante coped with losing his lucrative gambling business in Cuba, the U.S. was plotting to get rid of Fidel Castro. The CIA would supervise the project and give Castro the code name "The Beard."

In August, 1961, Richard Bissell, the CIA's Deputy Director for Plans, asked Sheffield Edwards, the CIA's Director of Security, if he could make contact with the Mafia that ran the gambling syndicate in Cuba. Bissell was a personal friend of President Kennedy, and many in the Federal government viewed him as the second most powerful man in the Kennedy Administration. Bissell headed the Agency's clandestine service and was responsible for a vast network of spies worldwide. Under Bissell's command, beginning in the late the 1950s, the Agency began to use bribery, propaganda and paramilitary force as tools of statecraft.

Edwards contacted Robert Maheu, a former FBI special agent and a private investigator who worked for the CIA, to find out if he had Mob connections. Maheu was reluctant to get involved with the anti- Castro project, although he did acknowledge having contacts who could give him access to the underworld. Edwards would not take no for an answer, and he pressured Maheu to change his mind. Maheu finally relented.

Maheu told Edwards that he would like to approach Johnny Roselli, a Los Angeles businessman with interests on the strip in Las Vegas. Maheu believed Roselli was a Mafia member.

Roselli also served as Chicago mobster's Sam Giancana's representative in Las Vegas. A friend of Trafficante, Sam "Momo" Giancana had used his Mafia influence to help John F. Kennedy become president in 1960. The mobster, it is believed, helped the Kennedy presidential campaign in Illinois in 1960 and at the request of family patriarch had raised money for Kennedy's crucial West Virginia campaign. Giancana also shared a girlfriend with the country's most powerful man, President John F Kennedy.

It is remarkable that the CIA would want to recruit a gangster like Sam Giancana. One police report described Giancana as a "snarling, sarcastic, foul-tongued, sadistic psychopath." His nickname "Momo" was a corruption of "mooner," which means a "nut case." Giancana had once put a contract out on entertainer Desi Arnaz because he produced "The Untouchables," which from Momo's point of view, had denigrated the Italian American Mafia, while lauding the Mafia's great nemesis Elliott Ness. Fortunately, cooler heads prevailed in the Mob and Giancana's contract was never executed. He was arrested more than 70 times and is believed responsible for numerous killings. Mob historian Carl Sifakis said Giancana qualified as "the most ruthless of the top bosses of organized crime."

Maheu arranged a meeting with Roselli in New York City on September 14, 1960, where he made the CIA's pitch. "Me?—You want me to get involved with Uncle Sam?" said an astonished Roselli when Maheu outlined the CIA plan. Roselli was reluctant to get involved. "The Feds are tailing me wherever I go, Bob. Are you sure you're talking to the right guy?" Maheu persisted and Roselli finally agreed to introduce Maheu to "Sam Gold," a code name for Sam Giancana, who either had or could arrange contacts with the Mafia clients who could do the job.

On September 28, 1960, Roselli and James P. O'Connell, a high- ranking CIA official, met with Sam Giancana at the Fontainbleau Hotel in Miami. Edwards authorized Maheu to tell Roselli that his clients would be willing to pay up to $150,000 for Castro's assassination.

It appeared, however, that good old fashion patriotism was the real reason that Roselli and Giancana got involved in the Castro assassination project. A memo written for the record by Sheffield Edwards on May 24, 1962 and now declassified stated: "No monies were ever paid to Roselli and Giancana. Maheu was paid part of his expense money during the periods he was in Miami." Maheu later recalled, "The truth as crazy as it may seem, is that deep down he (Roselli) thought it was his patriotic duty." Roselli had worked closely with Trafficante in the 1950s, and he late recruited the Tampa crime boss for the plot because of his knowledge of and numerous contacts in Cuba.

At the time, Trafficante was still making regular trips between Miami and Havana on Mob business, since the gambling casinos were still operating in Cuba. The casinos were closed on January 7, 1959, but six days later Castro announced that the casinos would be permitted to re-open for tourists and foreigners, but not Cubans. The casinos reopened in late February and were allowed to stay open until September, 1961. On one of his Cuba trips, Trafficante made arrangements with a contact inside Cuba to get the Castro assassination plot moving.

Long before the CIA contacted Roselli, it was considering a number of possible ways to get rid of Castro. At the time, Castro loved cigars and the Agency experimented with treating them with poisonous substances. The Agency considered contaminating a box of Castro's cigars with botulinum toxin, a virulent poison that produces a fatal illness if ingested. A 1967 CIA Inspector General's Report noted that "the cigars were so heavily contaminated that merely putting one in the mouth would do the job; the intended victim would not actually have to smoke it."

The CIA also looked at employing a shell-fish poison that could be administrated with aspirin or a handkerchief treated with bacteria and even putting a liquid poison in the tea, coffee or bouillon Castro drank frequently. Other schemes can only be characterized as hair brained. One involved blowing the Cuban leader out of the ocean while he was pursuing his passion for skin diving, while another would have infected Castro so that his beard would fall out, thus ruining his macho image.

The CIA also had the bright idea of arranging a typical gangland slaying in which Castro would be gunned down in a hail of bullets. Giancana and Roselli opposed the scheme, pointing out that hit men could not be recruited for the job because the chance for escape would virtually be nil.

Finally, CIA scientists developed a lethal pill it believed could do the job. Six of them were given to Trafficante, who delivered them to a man named Juan Orta. Trafficante assured the CIA that Orta had good access to Castro. Remarkably, while planning for the assassination was underway in Miami and Washington DC, the CIA did not know that Orta had lost his position in Cuba's prime minister's office on January 26, 1961, and had taken refuge in the Venezuelan Embassy on April 11, 1961. Orta did not get a safe conduct pass out of Cuba until October 1964.

A 1967 declassified CIA Inspector General's Report titled "Plots to Assassinate Fidel Castro" noted that "it seems likely that, while the Agency thought the gangsters had a man in Cuba with easy access to Castro, what they actually had was a man (Orta) disappointed at having lost access."

When the CIA realized the plot involving Orta would fail, Roselli told the CIA that Trafficante had a contact in the Cuban exile community who might be able to do the job. The man was Tony Varona, head of the anti Castro Democratic Revolutionary Front. Trafficante approached Varona and told him that Trafficante had clients who wanted to assassinate Castro and were willing to pay big money to someone who could do it. Varona was receptive because it would give him money to buy his own arms, boats and military supplies in his battle against Castro. According to a CIA Inspector General's report, the CIA paid Varona between $25,000 and $50,000.

The CIA gave money and the poison pills to Roselli, who passed them on to Varona. That was it. Incredibly, the CIA knew nothing from that point on about how Trafficante planned to have Castro killed. The Agency could only speculate. A press report said that Castro was ill, and the CIA concluded their assassination plan was working. But later, CIA intelligence learned that Castro was not really sick, and someone within the Agency speculated that Castro had planted stories in the press about his sickness because he knew in advance that the CIA was trying to kill him.

As time passed and nothing happened, the CIA never made the obvious conclusion: the Mafia was playing a con game. The mobsters the CIA had recruited had no real intention of killing the Cuban leader. They were simply telling their gullible spymasters what they wanted to hear. As Carl Sifakis described the situation: "… Trafficante was conning the intelligence agencies with thrilling tales of his men risking their lives, slipping into Cuba and having their boats shot out from under them." The stories, Roselli would later tell informer Jimmy "The Weasel" Fratianno, were "bullshit."

There is no evidence, moreover, that any of the money and/or equipment ever reached Cuba. Once again Trafficante was suspected of being an agent of Castro, revealing the CIA plots and feeding him information. After all, by doing so, Trafficante would be in a good position if Castro ever let the Mob back into Cuba.

The CIA plotting continued, as it planned for the invasion of Cuba and Castro's overthrow. The attack on Cuba would not involve U.S. troops, but would come from the CIA-trained Cuban exile community. The U.S. Air Force would provide the air cover. Meanwhile, relations with Cuba continued to deteriorate rapidly. In 1960, Cuba confiscated all U.S. investment and property on the island. In retaliation, Washington broke off diplomatic relations with Cuba in January 1961.

In the early morning of April 14, 1961, a squadron of U.S. B-26 bombers camouflaged with Cuban insignias began bombing airports in Cuba. Two days later, U.S. frogmen began landing on the beach of the Bay of Pigs and positioned themselves to guard the coming invasion. Brigade 2506, a group of 1200 Cubans spearheaded the invasion, but it turned into a total disaster and thousands of Cuban exiles were captured.

The plan was to have Castro's assassination coincide with the Bay of Pigs invasion. The CIA believed that Tony Varona had given the CIA poison pills to his contact in Cuba who awaited Varona's signal for him to use it. Meanwhile, the CIA put Varona under "protective custody" so the Agency could control the invasion's direction. In their book Ultimate Sacrifice, authors Lamar Waldron and Thom Hartmann noted: "the secret invasion could not be postponed even after it had become an open secret because it had to coincide with Castro's assassination." The authors con-cluded that "the CIA-Mafia plots were so tightly held within the CIA—known only to a handful of officials—that miscommunication resulted in the plot's failure."

The Bay of Pigs fiasco was not only a black day for the U.S. government and the Cuban exile community, but was also for the Mafia. Trafficante and his fellow mobsters viewed a successful Bay of Pigs invasion as their best way of getting back into Cuba. Trafficante who, despite the questions surrounding his relationship with Castro, maintained close relations with the Cuban community and was aware of the invasion plans. The godfather had no doubt the invasion would be a success, so he sent an aide to Nassau, Bahamas, where Trafficante kept a large amount of gold in a bank. Once the victorious invaders entered Havana, Trafficante's agent would follow with the gold, which would be used to re-open the casinos and get the gambling going again.

Sober reality quickly set in for the Mafia. It would not return triumphantly to Cuba. Instead, it became the target of a law and order investigation spearheaded by U.S. attorney General Robert Kennedy, JFK's brother. The FBI would place Trafficante under close surveillance for the rest of his life. The Mafia continued to work as hit men for the U.S. government, carrying out the assassination of Dominican dictator Rafael Trujillo, a month after the Bay of Pigs invasion. Trujillo had been the Dominican Republic's brutal dictator for 31 years. President Dwight D. Eisenhower feared that Trujillo's iron rule would spark a revolution modeled on what Fidel Castro had done in Cuba.

On May 30, 1961, Dominican exiles launched an invasion of the Dominican Republic from Cuba. The invasion failed miserably and the surviving rebels were rounded up by Trujillo's military, tortured and executed at a military base. But it was time for Trujillo to go. On May 30, 1961, assassins in a souped-up Chevy cut off Trujillo's car on an isolated stretch of highway in the Dominican Republic. They fired into Trujillo's car, killing him.

Later, Trujillo's bodyguard told reporters that the assassination involved Johnny Roselli. According to Waldron and Hartmann, Trujillo was killed in a hit very similar to one that Roselli's Chicago Mafia was famous for, the assassination of Mob boss Frankie Yale. Perhaps because of Roselli's success, the CIA continued to use Roselli and Trafficante in plots to assassinate Castro, but without telling the Kennedys.

4

UNDER PRESSURE

THE CIA'S TOP officials were not the only ones that might have been conned in the "Kill Castro" campaign. Trafficante and his associates realized they would not get a break from the U.S. government for their cooperation. Instead, the Kennedy Administration launched an all-out legal campaign against organized crime, led by Robert Kennedy, JFK's brother and the U.S. Attorney General.

The campaign had its roots in Robert Kennedy's tenure as chief counsel of the U.S. Senate Labor Rackets Committee, where he adopted an aggressive public posture in investigating organized crime. The Committee held hearings, which were televised, and Kennedy's tough questioning of witnesses made him a major national political figure.

Some of the country's leading mobsters—Joey Gallo, Tony Provenzano and Sam Giancana, for example—had to appear before the Committee. Sam Giancana, who had been a key member of the CIA's Castro assassination campaign, took the Fifth Amendment thirty-three times as Kennedy fired searing questions at him. For example:

Robert Kennedy: Would you tell us that if you have opposition from anybody, you dispose of them by having them stuffed in a trunk (sic). Is that what you do, Mr. Giancana?

Giancana: I decline to answer because I honestly believe any answer might tend to incriminate me.

Kennedy: Would you tell us anything about any of your operations or will you just giggle every time I ask you a question?

Giancana: I decline to answer because I honestly believe any answer might tend to incriminate me.

Kennedy: I thought only little girls giggled, Mr. Giancana.

Giancana and his Mob associates considered the Kennedys to be hypocrites because they knew that the patriarch of the family, Joseph P. Kennedy, had made his fortune in part through bootleg whiskey during Prohibition. According to Mob historian James Mannion, Joe Kennedy's ties with the Mob continued after Prohibition. Papa Kennedy also was a heavy gambler, a part owner of a racetrack, and an associate of such leading crime figures as Meyer Lansky and Frank Costello.

Trafficante knew that Robert's brother, John, the president of the world's most powerful country, was sharing the pleasures of a woman named Judith Campbell Exner with fellow mobster Sam Giancana, who had met Exner through Frank Sinatra. In 1978, Exner revealed that she had acted as a courier between Giancana and Kennedy, carrying sealed envelopes for them on at least ten occasions.

In one of the hearings most dramatic moments, Robert Kennedy squared off with Teamsters Union president Jimmy Hoffa, at the time perhaps the country's most powerful union officials. The Committee had instructed Kennedy, as its chief counsel, to collect information on Hoffa. While doing so, he found several financial irregularities and at the hearings, he challenged Hoffa with the evidence.

Hoffa had ties with the Mafia, and some sources believe he was part of the CIA-Mafia nexus. Dan Moldea, in his book The Hoffa Wars: the Rise and Fall of Jimmy Hoffa, contends that "strong evidence points to the fact that the original middleman between the CIA and the American underworld was Jimmy Hoffa, who used the union's financial machinery for arms sales to both sides of the Cuban revolution." Moldea revealed

that a Hoffa aide who later became a government informant believed his boss was the initial
go-between the CIA and the Mob in the Castro
assassination plot.   Kennedy created a specific
Hoffa unit in its Justice Department to pursue
and hound Jimmy Hoffa whom the Attorney
General suspected had robbed the Teamster's
Union pension plan.

FBI Director J. Edgar Hoover had inad-
vertently contributed to the Mafia's growth by
denying its existence. But when John F. Kennedy
appointed his brother U.S. Attorney General,
Robert pushed Hoover to do more. Consequent-
ly, the number of organized crime convictions
jumped from a mere 35 in 1960 to 288 in 1963.

Robert Kennedy also went after Carlo Marcello, the powerful New Orleans based mobster
who was a friend of Santo Trafficante. At 5'3",
Marcello was known as the "Little Man," but like
Trafficante, he was a ruthless and a shrewd opera-
tor. Born Calogero Minacore in 1910 in Tunis,
North Africa, Marcello's Sicilian parents brought
him to the U.S when he was eight months old.
Marcello never became a citizen.

By 1947, Marcello had taken over the gambling rackets in Louisiana. In climbing to the top
of the underworld, he was arrested for robbery,
tax evasion, aggravated assault, gambling and
drug trafficking. As Marcello grew in power, he
became known for not only killing his enemies,

but also soaking their bodies in lye and then burying them on his 6,500-acre private estate outside of New Orleans

Marcello appeared at the Kefauver Hearings in January 1951, but, in true godfather fashion, refused to say anything more than his name, address and the usual spiel that answering any and all questions might tend to incriminate him. Marcello was found guilty of contempt of Congress and sentenced to six months in prison. Marcello appealed and won, but his troubles were not over. He had been convicted of marijuana possession, and a 1952 law made that a deportable offense. U.S. Immigration officials warned Marcello that he could be subject to deportation from the U.S.

By the 1950s, police and media were calling Marcello the head of organized crime in Louisiana and along the Mississippi coast, although he kept insisting he was nothing more than a tomato salesman. By the early 1960s, Marcello was fighting a losing battle with U.S authorities who were trying to deport him.

On April 4, 1961, less than a month after Robert Kennedy had been sworn in as Attorney General, Federal officials told Marcello that he was a citizen of Guatemala, and they then put him on a plane to that country. The reason Uncle Sam deported the mobster to Guatemala-- a birth certificate bearing his name was found in the Guatemalan village of San Jose Pinula.

Marcello spent a month there before moving first to San Salvador and then to Honduras. Two months later, he was back in the U.S., much to the dismay and shock of the U.S. government. How he got back still remains a mystery.

So Marcello had ample reason to kill the Kennedys. Sources also revealed more about Marcello to U.S. law enforcement. They talked about a September 1962 meeting at Marcello's farm, during which, in reference to Robert Kennedy, Marcello blurted: "Get the stone out of the shoe." It was a well-known Sicilian curse. One source, who claimed to have attended the meeting, said Marcello screamed: "Don't worry about that little Bobby son-of-a-bitch. He's going to be taken care of."

Marcello also reportedly talked about setting up a patsy to take the blame for JFK's assassination. "That's the way they do it all the time in Sicily," Marcello said. Interestingly, it is believed the Marcello crime syndicate knew Lee Harvey Oswald through David Ferrie, a quirky private investigator who lost all his hair to a rare disease and wore lousy looking Mohawk hairpieces and fake eyebrows. In Oliver Stone's movie about the JFK assassination, actor Joe Pesci played David Ferrie.

Trafficante did not hide his friendship with Marcello. In testifying before House Select Committee on Assassinations in 1978, Trafficante recalled: "I know Carlos Marcello about 30 years. I had met him in New Orleans. My father had an operation there." Trafficante admitted that he had conversations with Marcello about Bobby Kennedy and how he had Marcello deported to Guatemala. Trafficante also revealed that he felt "Robert Kennedy had mistreated Marcello." Uncle Sam was also pursuing and investigating Santo Trafficante, Jr. In June 1959, The Washington Post reported that Trafficante and his wife, Josephine, as well as his brother Sam and sister-in-law Elsie, settled a $200,747 tax claim (forty cents on the dollar) with the IRS. The IRS charged them with operating an "illegal gambling business."

The IRS claimed Trafficante, Jr. and his wife had under estimated their income by $91,587 for the years 1954 and 1955; and charged Junior with filing false and fraudulent income tax returns, as well as failure to keep accurate records. Trafficante denied the claims and contended that the government had incorrectly calculated extra income and wrongly charged them with intent to evade taxes.

Like Marcello, Trafficante said things about JFK that could be interpreted as threatening or foreshadowing. Jose Aleman, a prominent member of the Cuban exile community with strong Mafia ties, told U.S. government authorities about a meeting he had with Santo Trafficante at a hotel in Washington, DC, in September 1962. Aleman's grandfather had reportedly been a lawyer for Luciano, and according to authors Lamar Waldron and Thom Hartmann, "Aleman's family had really helped Jimmy Hoffa gain control of a Miami Bank that Hoffa could use to launder money for his criminal activities. The Aleman family had been rich in land holdings before the Cuban revolution, but had fallen on hard times in its exile in the U.S."

Aleman was in debt, but the authors noted: "His contacts could still be of use to someone like Trafficante who was always looking for seemingly legitimate funds for money-laundering and other scams." According to The Washington Post, in one of their three meetings, Trafficante offered to arrange a million dollar loan for Aleman from the Teamster's Union funds, a move that Hoffa had already approved.

At his meeting with Aleman, Trafficante was waxing philosophically about democracy, socialism and communism when he brought up Jimmy Hoffa's name. Hoffa, Trafficante mused, would never forgive the Kennedys for what they did to him. He then added; "Mark my word, this man Kennedy is in trouble and he will get what is coming to him."

Aleman disagreed with Trafficante and said Kennedy would never get re-elected. Trafficante answered: "You don't understand me. Kennedy is not going to make it to the election. He is going to be hit."

The U.S. government's campaign against the Mafia came to national attention on January 21, 1962, when famed investigative journalist Jack Anderson wrote a story in Parade magazine about Operation Big Squeeze, the code name the federal authorities gave to its anti-Mafia campaign. "The full force of the Federal Government had been thrown into the battle against it (the Mafia)," Anderson predicted. In dramatic language, Anderson described how the government had "the racketeers on the run. From plush penthouses to lush ranch houses, over the radio phone from one Cadillac to another, the word had gone out; the heat is on."

In the article, Anderson chronicled the Mob's recent history: the Kefauver Commission hearings, the 1957 Apalachin Conference, the Mafia's influence in pre revolutionary Cuba and the hit on Albert Anastasia. Anderson revealed how Trafficante had "tried in vain to do business with Cuba" and provided more evidence that Castro's rise to power had bankrupted the godfather. He wrote that Trafficante had tried to dispose of a reported $22 million in Cuban currency, which Castro suddenly outlawed. The gangster tried to peddle his huge cache for as little as 12 cents on the dollar. But the last report from the underworld was that he is stuck with millions of worthless bills."

Anderson provided a chart of "The Top Ten" mobsters in the U.S., which included Santo Trafficante, whom Anderson described as "dangerous and dignified" at number ten. However, Carlo Marcello was not included. The conclusion of Anderson's expose: "The Justice Department doesn't expect Operation Big Squeeze to produce similar and dramatic results. Organized crime is largely entrenched, has vast resources. But the American public, so long held to ransom by the racketeers, should be glad to know that the squeeze is on."

This expose must have put to rest any illusion that Trafficante and his fellow mobsters had about getting back to "business as usual" while JFK was president and his brother was the country's top law enforcement official. Trafficante was certainly feeling the heat of the federal probe. In a conversation overheard in a Miami restaurant, Trafficante complained bitterly about the U.S. government's anti- organized crime campaign and how his gambling establishments were being targeted. The pressure was intense, Trafficante revealed, lamenting cryptically, "I know when I'm beat, you understand?"

Meanwhile, the Attorney General's investigation was intensifying. Nine months after Jack Anderson's article appeared, Edward Grady

Partin, a Teamsters official in Baton Rouge, Louisiana, approached Robert Kennedy's office with an offer of information of a "security nature." Partin had been indicted two months previously on 26 counts of embezzlement and falsification of union records, and he was looking for a deal. Partin told Justice Department officials that Hoffa had tried to bribe members of federal grand jury in Nashville. The grand jury had refused to indict Hoffa on an illegal pay off scheme, but did indict him on the charge of jury tampering and convicted him on May 9, 1963.

During this period, the events leading to that fateful day in November 1963 in Dallas were moving inexorably to their conclusion. On September 28, Lee Harvey Oswald boarded a bus in Nuevo Laredo, Texas, for Mexico City. Upon arriving, he visited the Cuban Embassy to get a visa, but then officials told him it would take four months to get one. Furious, Oswald stormed out of the Cuban Embassy and walked the short distance to the Russian Embassy, where he again applied for a visa, but was delayed once again. On September 30 he tried both embassies again without success.

The same day, the frustrated Oswald bought a bus ticket back to the U.S., and four days later, Oswald arrived in Dallas, Texas. On October 15, he applied and was hired for a job at the Texas School Book Depository (TSDBD). At this time

FBI agent James Hostig began to investigate Oswald and make inquiries about him. On November 12, Oswald walked into the FBI building in Dallas and delivered a note that was addressed to Hostig: "Leave my family alone," Oswald demanded.

In October, President Kennedy decided to visit Dallas, but local officials had concerns about his safety. On October 24, the U.S. Ambassador to the UN, Adlai Stevenson had been jostled, spit upon and struck by a protest sign while visiting Dallas. To ensure similar problems would not arise during President Kennedy's visit, the City of Dallas prepared the most stringent security precautions in its history.

On November 22, Oswald entered the TSBD with a package. He was seen looking toward the motorcade route of President Kennedy. At 12:30 p.m. Kennedy, while driving in a presidential motorcade within Dealey Plaza, was fatally wounded by gunshots. At 1:40 p.m., Oswald was captured in the Texas Theater after a struggle with police. During his flight, Oswald had shot Dallas Police officer J.D. Tippit. The police questioned Oswald and formally arraigned him for Tippit's murder.

At 11:26 p.m., Oswald was charged with Kennedy's murder. The complaint stated: "Lee Harvey Oswald, in furtherance of an international communist conspiracy, assassinated President John F. Kennedy." At the time, many believed JFK's assassination had Cold War overtones.

Oswald was interrogated for two days, but he never confessed. On November 23, the police announced that they would transfer Oswald to the community jail the next morning at 10 a.m. On November 24 at 10:21 a.m., Jack Ruby, acting and sounding like character out of an old Jimmy Cagney movie, shot Oswald, shouting, "You killed my president, you rat." The police tackled Ruby and arrested him.

Ruby knew the Sam and Joe Campisi brothers, who were leading figures in the Dallas underworld and close associates of none other than Carlo Marcello. The Campisi brothers visited Ruby in private while he was in jail, raising suspicions that Oswald had been the target of a Mob hit. Later, after his trial for killing Oswald, Ruby told the press that "Everything pertaining to what's happening has never come to the surface. The world will never know the true facts of what occurred, my motives."

In Miami, Trafficante wanted to celebrate when he heard the news. He had planned to meet lawyer Frank Ragano-- and Ragano's girlfriend-- for dinner at Tampa's International Inn, where, ironically, JFK had given a speech four days earlier. Ragano later recalled, "In the same hotel lobby I was crossing to meet Santo, Kennedy had shaken hands and waved at admirers earlier in the week."

Ragano described what happened when Trafficante appeared: "A smiling Santo greeted me at our table. Isn't that something? They killed that son-of-a-bitch." The godfather hugged and kissed his lawyer's cheeks. "Trafficante's generally bland face was wreathed in joy," said Ragano, who recalled Trafficante saying, "This is like lifting a load of stones off my shoulders…. now they'll get off my back, off Carlo's back and off Hoffa's back. We'll make big money out of this and maybe get back into Cuba. I'm glad for Hoffa's sake because Lyndon Johnson is sure as hell going to remove Bobby. I don't see how he'll keep him in office."

When Ragano's girlfriend arrived and the waiter brought her a drink, Trafficante made a toast: "For a hundred years of health and to John Kennedy's death." Upset by the remark, Ragano's girlfriend "banged her glass on the table and rushed out of the restaurant," Ragano recalled. According to the lawyer, his ecstatic client and friend "continued toasting in Sicilian to the beautiful times he was certain were coming."

On the day of JFK's assassination, Marcello's trial was in progress. At 1:30 p.m. CST, two hours after the mega event, a bailiff marched into the courtroom and delivered a note to the judge. Visibly shaken, the judge announced to the court that the President had been shot and might be dead. The judge called for an hour's recess. At 3 p.m., fifteen minutes after the court-resumed session, the jury delivered its verdict. Marcello was not guilty on both counts of perjury and conspiracy

Frank Ragano revealed that Jimmy Hoffa called him to gloat over the news, but Hoffa's mood changed after he got a call from a Teamsters official in Washington. Hoffa was furious that Teamsters leaders at the Union's headquarters had closed the office, lowered its flag half mast and sent condolences to the president's widow. "Hoffa yelled at his secretary for crying, hung up on the people in Washington and left the building," according to Ragano.

Lyndon Baines Johnson took the oath of office as president at 2:38 p.m. on November 22, the day of the assassination. Seven days later, he created the President's Commission on the Assassination of John F. Kennedy, the so-called Warren Commission. In addition to Earl Warren, Chief Justice of the U.S. Supreme Court, commission members included U.S. Senators Richard B., Russell (D-Georgia), John Sherman Cooper (R-Kentucky), U.S. Representative Hale Boggs (D-Louisiana) and Gerald R. Ford (R-Michigan), Allen. W. Dulles, former CIA Director, and John J. McCoy, former World Bank president. The Commission named former U.S. Solicitor General James Lee Rankin as its general counsel, and it appointed 14 assistant counselors and an additional staff of 12. Given unrestricted investigative powers, the Commission was charged with evaluating all the evidence collected in JFK's assassination and presenting a complete report to the American people.

The Commission heard the testimony of 512 witnesses and read the reports of ten Federal agencies. The hearings, however, were closed to the public unless the person giving the testimony requested otherwise. Only two witnesses made such a request.

The Commission relied solely on the FBI to do the investigative work, and later the Commission acknowledged that the FBI, as well as the CIA, did not provide it with all the evidence those agencies had collected. In total, the published files of the Warren Commission came to 26 volumes.

In its final report, which was delivered to President Johnson on September 24, 1964, the Commission reached the conclusions that have been hotly debated ever since. The Commission found:

No evidence that Oswald was involved with any person or group in a conspiracy to assassinate the President.

No evidence that anyone assisted Oswald in planning or carrying out the assassination

Then it made its most stunning conclusion: "On the basis of the evidence before the Commission, it concludes that Oswald acted alone."

The idea that a lone gunman had assassinated the President of the United States, the world's most powerful individual, would be difficult for many Americans to accept. In the years ahead, the CIA, the Mafia, the Cuban exile community, and Castro himself would all be accused of plotting the assassination. And at the center of the controversy would be Tampa mobster, Santo Trafficante, Jr.

Cuba played a big role in Trafficante's mobster career

Fidel Castro—Trafficante was believed to be involved with CIA plots to kill Castro

Johnny Roselli was a close associate of Santo Trafficante, Jr.

Santo Trafficante (middle) with close associate Carlo Marcello (l) and his lawyer Frank Ragano

Santo Trafficante Jr., like many other leading mobsters, developed a hatred of President John F. Kennedy

CG 92-349

REFERENCES: Report of SA ███ dated 8/25/59 at Chicago.
(Continued)   Report of SA ███ dated 10/21/59 at Chicago.
                 Report of SA ███ dated 12/28/59 at Chicago.
(b)(7)(c)   Report of SA ███ dated 2/18/60 at Chicago.
                 Report of SA ███ dated 4/6/60
                 at Chicago.
                 Report of SA ███ dated 5/26/60 at Chicago.
                 Report of SA ███ dated 7/29/60
                 at Chicago.
                 Bureau airtel to Chicago dated 8/26/60.

- P -

LEAD

CHICAGO

AT CHICAGO, ILLINOIS. Will continue to follow and
report on the activities of SAMUEL M. GIANCANA.

ADMINISTRATIVE

(b)(2)   The information contained herein is that which was
(b)(7)(D)   obtained from ███, a highly confidential source. This
                information covers the period from approximately August 1, 1959
                through September 1, 1960. This information will tend to reveal
                to some degree GIANCANA's position in the Chicago crime syndicate
                and to a lesser degree his associates, legitimate enterprises,
                tie-ins with politics and police.

(b)(2)   EXTREME CAUTION SHOULD BE USED IN THE EVENT INFORMATION
(b)(7)(D)   FURNISHED BY ███ IS UTILIZED IN ANY FUTURE INVESTIGATION.
                IN THE EVENT SUCH INFORMATION IS USED, ALL EFFORTS TO ADEQUATELY
                PROTECT THIS SOURCE SHOULD BE UTILIZED INCLUDING APPROPRIATE
                PARAPHRASING.

COVER PAGE

- A1 -

Page from Sam Giancana's FBI file (self explanatory)

Sam Giancana, powerful Chicago mobster, was an associate of Santo Trafficante, Jr,

Santo Trafficante Jr., Godfather of the Tampa Mafia

5
UNDER SURVEILLANCE

TRAFFICANTE'S MOB TIES came to public light in the fall of 1963 when Joseph Valachi appeared before the McClellan Committee. Valachi, a long-time Mafia member, was the first Mob informant to get national attention. He was a soldier in Salvatore's Maranzano's Mob family in the 1920s; in 1930 became a made man, which meant he became an official member of the Italian American Mafia. When the dust settled from the Castellammarese War, Valachi joined Lucky Luciano's crime family, eventually reporting to Vito Genovese.

During his long criminal career, Valachi worked hard for the Mob as an enforcer, hit man, drug trafficker and numbers runner, but he was convicted of a drug charge in 1959 and was sent to an Atlanta prison to serve a 15- to 20-year sentence. Ironically, Valachi found himself in a jail cell with his old boss Vito Genovese.

The godfather mistakenly suspected Valachi of being an informant, and gave him the "kiss of death," a Mafia ritual that meant Valachi's days in the Mafia were numbered. Valachi feared for his life and thought the Mob had sent someone—a prisoner--to kill him. Believing the hit man was a fellow prisoner, Valachi took preventive action and clubbed the one he suspected to death with an iron bar. He killed the wrong man, and his prison sentence was increased from 15 to 20 years to life.

When the Mob put a $100,000 contract on his life, Valachi decided to tell all to the authorities, and in 1962 he turned informant. Valachi became one of the most valuable federal witnesses ever, compelling the U.S. government to put Valachi in the Federal Witness Protection program and to guard him with up to 200 U.S. marshals.

In his nationally televised appearance before the McClellan Committee, Valachi formally identified 317 organized crime members, including Santo Trafficante. During the hearings, Trafficante's photo appeared at the top of a chart depicting the organizational structure of the Tampa crime family. Santo liked to keep a low profile, but the American public now knew him as one of the country's most important mobsters.

But by the time Valachi testified, the FBI already knew that Santo Trafficante, Jr. was a major force in the Mafia. The Bureau had him under constant surveillance while it gathered intelligence on him. The FBI's Tampa field office was opened in 1960 to monitor the Tampa Mafia. Joseph F. Santoima headed the office until his retirement in 1973 after 33 years of service with the Bureau. Under Santoima's leadership, the Tampa office spent considerable resources monitoring Santo Trafficante, Jr. Wherever the godfather went, the FBI was sure to follow, and they had no problem letting its target know it.

Files released under the Freedom of Information Act (FOIA) reveal that the FBI's field offices in Miami and Tampa played the major role in the surveillance. For nearly three decades, the field offices kept voluminous files, containing memos, reports, newspaper clippings, telegrams, coded messages and other records. In all the FBI collected more than 38,000 pages of information on Trafficante.

The intelligence gathering began in earnest about 1958 when Alberto Anastasia was shot to death as he sat in a barber's chair in New York City. The files confirm that Trafficante had been at Anastasia's dinner partner the night before and that Trafficante had checked out of the hotel two hours before Anastasia was hit. The files cover Trafficante's days in pre-revolutionary war Cuba, including his arrest and incarceration in Trescornia prison, which, the field reports noted, was more Club Med than Alcatraz. As the files reveal, Trafficante's family and friends could bring food in and even enjoy entertainment with the prisoner.

The St. Petersburg Times newspaper, which got the Freedom of Information Act (FOIA) files released, reported that FBI agents tailing Trafficante often recorded the mileage of his Dodge Dart or Chevy whenever they found the cars unattended. Agents would look inside Trafficante's car even though they did not have a warrant. One time, agents found four sealed thank-you notes, a bank envelope and a car service center receipt, indicating that Trafficante had paid $110 for four Atlas tires.

The FBI was a stickler for detail. For instance, in one 1966 report, an agent spent considerable space in a report describing how Trafficante got a flat tire on a trip to Miami. His report recorded that it took him from 3:10 p.m. to 3:24 p.m. to change the Dodge Dart's front left tire.

The authorities were interested in every little detail of Trafficante's life and in every move he made. In making his report for August 21, 1961, narcotics agent Oscar Leon Davis wrote that on his most recent visit to Miami, Trafficante purchased a pair of contact lenses and twelve pairs of prescription glasses, all with different frames. Davis wrote: "The Miami Police Department's Intelligence Unit is of the opinion that the purchase of those glasses of different frames could be that he wishes to change his appearance or that he plans to leave the country and wants to take an ample supply with him."

No part of Trafficante's life was out of bounds for the FBI's investigation. For instance, when Trafficante's wife was hospitalized at Tampa's St. Joseph's hospital in 1966, the agents tailed the godfather on his daily visits to see her.

The agents would follow him to the airport where they watched him buy newspapers before boarding a plane. Trafficante would sometimes try and shake the FBI tail by buying the airline tickets under an assumed name. On one occasion, he exhibited a sense of humor using the name of the agent who was following him to purchase a ticket. But files show that the FBI seemed to know when Trafficante was scheduled to return to Tampa. When his plane landed, they would pick him up the surveillance and continue tailing him once again, as he made his daily rounds about Tampa before returning to his home on Bristol Street.

Trafficante would also play games with FBI agents by talking in Italian when he knew they were nearby trying to ease drop on his conversations. Apparently, none of the agents tailing him understood Italian.

But on one occasion the normally low-key mobster blew his top. In 1967, the local police met

Trafficante at the Miami International Airport and told him that he was no longer welcome in South Florida. A livid Trafficante shouted at the police officers after they asked for identification: "You sons of a bitch! You can't do this to me. This isn't Russia!" As a Miami Herald reporter and a photographer looked on, Trafficante was arrested and charged with vagrancy, disorderly conduct and possession of drugs, which turned out to be diet pills his doctor had prescribed.

According to Tampa Mob historian Scott M. Deitche, "This was just one of many examples of the bullish tactics law enforcement used in their attempts to rattle mobsters under their surveillance." The police eventually dropped the charges when Trafficante's lawyer, Frank Ragano, threatened legal action after a photo of his client appeared in The Miami Herald. Trafficante did sue the Miami police for $1 in damages for violating his civil rights, but the lawsuit got tied up in the courts, and the mobster eventually dropped it.

J. Edgar Hoover was made aware that the Trafficante surveillance had the potential for legal problems. In 1967 he wrote a memo to his Tampa and Miami field offices, warning his agents to be "circumspect and discrete…so there can be no basis for any allegations of harassment and to avoid, in so far as possible, any attacks on the FBI's investigative procedures by the hoodlums and their attorneys."

The FBI's Trafficante investigation, however, was hampered by internal struggles within the FBI over who would be responsible for the surveillance. Eventually, the surveillance was split, with the Tampa office responsible for central Florida and the Miami office for the South Florida area.

As part of its intelligence gathering operation, the FBI read the local newspaper regularly for any news about Trafficante's activities. This included weekly wedding announcements and funeral notices. "Whenever a paper in Tampa, St. Petersburg or Miami wrote about Trafficante, the FBI would immediately wire the story to other FBI field offices nationwide," The St. Petersburg Times revealed. One newspaper article from the file described Trafficante as a Tampa mobster whose "influence extended throughout Florida."

Despite the intense surveillance, Trafficante tried to carry on with business as usual. On September 22, 1966, he was attending a Mob meeting at the La Stella Italian restaurant in Queens, New York, when two NYPD officers walked in. Trafficante was in the company of some of the city's biggest crime bosses, including Carlo Gambino, boss of the Gambino crime family; Joe Colombo, boss of the Profaci crime family, Thomas Eboli, boss of the Genovese crime family, and Carlos Marcello and his brother Joe of New Orleans.

"What's the meeting about?" the police officers asked the gathering.

Marcello answered: "I decided to see some of my old friends so we all got together for lunch. Sure, some of these fellows have been in the rackets, but if they're in the Mafia, I don't know a damn thing about that. This was strictly a social gathering. That's all there was to it."

The powerful godfathers were meeting, the authorities learned later, to decide who would be the big godfather in New Orleans. Carlos Marcello controlled the scene, but Anthony Carolla, an ambitious up-and-coming scion of a New Orleans godfather, wanted a bigger share of the action. The Mafia had actually made their decision in favor of Carlos Marcello at an earlier meeting, and this was, as Marcello said, a social gathering.

The police officers, however, did not like the answer, and they arrested the 13 men present at the meeting. The charge-- consorting with known criminals. They were taken to a local police precinct, stripped down to their underwear, fingerprinted and held on $100,000 bond. The mobsters were subpoenaed to appear before a grand jury, but each of them invoked the Fifth Amendment. Unable to bring any charges that would stick, the police had to release them. Undeterred, Trafficante and Marcello consorted once again by going to lunch together the afternoon of their release.

Trafficante was allowed to return to Florida, but he had to travel to New York five times to appear before a grand jury. In true godfather fashion, he said nothing to the jury except when he invoked the Fifth Amendment.

In October 1967, another grand jury began hearings into organized crime's relationship with Tampa's liquor industry. Several suspected mobsters, including members of the Trafficante crime family, had to appear before the panel. All of them invoked the Fifth Amendment or gave evasive answers. Trafficante took the Fifth 80 times. On October 26, 1967, the grand jury indicted Frank Albano, the son-in-law of Santos' brother Sam, and one of Santo's brothers, Henry Trafficante. The court charged the defendants with unlawfully labeling liquor bottles and released them on $76,500 bail.

The authorities were trying to rattle the Tampa crime boss and to force him into making a mistake, but they were not succeeding. Despite the close surveillance, Trafficante continued to travel the country on Mob business. A July 10, 1968 Dade County OCB memo noted that he had traveled to Hong Kong, Thailand and other

Asian countries and that various intelligence sources were fairly certain that a large scale narcotics operation was the reason.

An informant advised the OCB that on July 8, 1968, Trafficante had visited the residence of Evaristo Garcia and advised him to be careful in moving ahead with the plans for Ecuador. Trafficante told Garcia that a ten million dollar deal had "fallen through." That remark about their Ecuador plans, the OCB speculated, most likely referred to the proposed construction of a casino at Guayaquil, Ecuador, which was to be used as a center for organized crime activities in Latin America.

The FBI began investigating the disappearance of an associate of Trafficante named Luigi Pietro Coliachin, also known as Louis P. Brady. A FBI report noted that a special agent of the FBI's Miami office last saw Brady on August 9, 1963. Brady's wife, Frances, told the FBI that she had last been with her husband at the Capra Restaurant in Miami Beach. The Bradys and their son were dining with friends, awaiting Santo Trafficante, who telephoned to say he would be arriving shortly. Before that happened, though, Brady sent his family home. The wife never saw her husband again. In its report, the FBI noted: "Mrs. Brady is of the opinion that Trafficante is responsible for her husband's disappearance."

The intelligence reports show that the authorities were certainly aware of Trafficante's movements and activities, but it did not seem to make a difference. Despite all the information being collected, they were still far from building a solid case against the mobster. As the 1960s came to a close, the authorities were no closer to nabbing the Tampa godfather than they were a decade before when their surveillance first began.

6
GETTING AT THE TRUTH

IN 1968, THE Federal authorities began a major initiative to investigate Tampa organized crime. First, Santo Trafficante, his brother Henry Trafficante, Nick Scaglione, Johnny Rivera and other leading local mobsters, were called before a grand jury formed to investigate the 1953 murder of Henry Hicks. Hicks was a janitor at the Silver Metro Bar in Tampa who was killed when buckshot, intended for mobster Paul Ferraro, hit Hicks in the face.

Another grand jury probe looked into Tampa's gambling scene and liquor industry, while still another began investigating the ties between organized crime and the Port of Tampa. Two years later, the grand jury ordered Santo Trafficante to appear at the trial of his brother Fano and his son-in-law Frank Albano. They faced charges resulting from their 1967 arrest for

unlawfully labeling liquor bottles and watering
down drinks at one of the family-owned bars, a
violation of federal law.

When the authorities came to Santo's house
to deliver the subpoena, August Piniello, Santo's
son-in-law, told them that Trafficante was not
home. The godfather was actually in the back-
room and did not want to come out. After the
Feds left, Trafficante sent a message to the FBI's
Tampa office asking that the subpoena be re-sent.
The Feds did not want to play games, and they
came back to the house and arrested

Trafficante and his son–in-law for obstruction of justice. The charge was only a misdemean-
or, but given Trafficante's notoriety, the incident
received a lot of publicity.

The morning that Trafficante testified before
the grand jury, the jury foreman received a threatening call. The media speculated that Trafficante
might have been behind the call, but he denied
having anything to do with it. Trafficante did
plead guilty, though, to the obstruction of justice
charge, and he was sentenced to one-year probation, contingent upon him finding a job. This
Trafficante did when he went to work as a sales
representative for DeRojatis Fashions in Miami.

It seemed that the godfather was spending as
much time in court as he was running his criminal empire. In 1971, another federal grand jury
probing possible corruption in local government

subpoenaed Trafficante. Son-in-law Frank Albino was given immunity from prosecution, but he did not give investigators any information of substance.

These grand juries were minor affairs compared to the grand jury convened in 1975 to investigate the murder of 37-year Tampa police detective Richard Cloud. The killing outraged Tampa, and the federal and local agencies put enormous pressure on informants, while they combed the underworld looking for leads.

Cloud, one of Tampa's most respected police officers, had been investigating organized crime's relationship with the local narcotics trade. Cloud was focusing on Joe Bedami, Jr., and Cloud had gathered enough evidence to bring charges against the alleged mobster and put him away for a long time. Cloud was also collecting evidence about possible police corruption relating to drug investigations. But in March 1975, Cloud and two other officers were accused of physically abusing two suspects in a police parking lot. Cloud's supervisors learned of the incident and ordered him to take a lie detector test. When Cloud refused, the police department fired him.

Cloud had an excellent professional reputation, and he had no problem finding another job in law enforcement. He began work as a consultant on organized crime for the Federal government, while continuing his investigation of possible corruption in the police department from which he was fired. One morning in October 1975, Cloud answered the doorbell of his modest Tampa home to find two gunmen waiting; one shot him in the chest. Cloud fell to the floor and the gunmen shot him five more times, hitting Cloud in the leg and abdomen, before fleeing in a late model green and black Dodge Charger.

Neighbors heard the shots and called police. An ambulance rushed Cloud to the hospital, but he was pronounced dead on arrival. The only evidence found at the scene where spent 32-caliber bullets and their shell casings.

The murder shocked Tampa and put the public spotlight on its police department. Cloud's friends believed he had collected enough damaging evidence on two police officers in the department; in a press interview, some of Cloud's friends recalled him saying: "I have enough on them to end their careers."

The police put Cloud's files in a safe place and announced that they planned to subpoena suspected underworld figures like Santo and Henry Trafficante to find out who killed Cloud. Once again, Tampa's leading godfather was under investigation for murder. A grand jury was convened the day after Cloud's death. The police did not get a lead in the Cloud investigation until January 1976 when a suspicious landlord told them about a boarder who was obsessive about the Cloud case and wanted to know every little detail about it. The boarder was Benjamin Roy Gilford, an escapee from state prison. The police investigated and arrested Gilford for Cloud's murder. In interrogation, Gilford gave up one of his accomplices, Eddie Haskew.

Mobster Victor Acosta, it turned out, hired the hit men, but before the police could bring him in for questioning, he fled Tampa. The Cloud investigation led to a big racketeering indictment that marked a turning point for the Tampa Mob. According to Tampa Mafia historian Scott Deitche, "Many of the younger mobsters who were looking to move into the rackets found themselves under siege from the law, and many of them were taken out of the business before they had a chance to get started. It also gave investigators new intelligence insight into the Mob's operations in the area."

By the mid 1970s, at the time of the Cloud murder investigation, Santo Trafficante had become a mobster, who, to paraphrase legendary boxer Joe Louis, could run but not hide. It had been common knowledge that Trafficante had been heavily involved in the CIA campaign to assassinate Castro, but Congress had done little to investigate that involvement. However, in the wake of the Watergate scandal that broke in 1973 and brought down Richard Nixon's presidential administration, Congress was willing to flex its power and to take steps to investigate possible illegal government activities.

The movement for an investigation of covert government activities gained impetus in December 1974 when noted investigative journalist Seymour Hersh published an article in The New York Times exposing the U.S. government's covert program to kill foreign leaders and subvert foreign governments. The article also revealed that U.S. intelligence agencies were collecting information on political activities of U.S. citizens.

The following month, the U.S. Senate established the United States Select Committee to Study Governmental Operations with Regards to Intelligence Activities, more commonly known as the Church Committee. Named after Senator Frank Church (D-Idaho), the Committee was charged to hold hearings as part of a wide-ranging investigation of the intelligence agencies in the post-Watergate period. A big part of the Committee's work involved looking into plots to kill the following former foreign leaders: Patrice Lumumba (Congo), Rafael Trujillo (Dominican Republic) Ngu Dinh Diem (Vietnam) and Rene Schneider (Chile).

The Church Committee was keenly interested in investigating possible CIA-Mafia links, but two important witnesses never made it to Capitol Hill to testify. On a muggy Chicago

June evening in 1975, Sam Giancana was fixing a midnight snack of Italian sausage, spinach and beans in the basement kitchen of his suburban Oak Park, Illinois home; the sausages were still simmering when the caretaker found the 66-year old mobster lying face down in a pool of blood. He had been shot once in the mouth and five times in the face. The gun used in the slaying was later traced to Florida. When investigating the scene later, authorities noted that Giancana had opened the metal door, leading to the stairway and backyard, to let some one in. Giancana must have known the killer, the authorities concluded.

Giancana's murder baffled law enforcement. He had been all but retired for years from the Mafia, and the 22-caliber pistol that killed him was not the type of gun usually used in Mafia hits. There was a rumor, though, that the mobster would be testifying before the Church Committee. Giancana knew much about where all the dead bodies were buried, especially when it came to the CIA-Mob connection, and there was speculation that sinister forces wanted him dead.

In July 1976, Johnny Roselli had dinner with Trafficante at a seafood restaurant in Fort Lauderdale. The two mobsters reminisced about old times and the upcoming Church Committee hearings. Roselli was scheduled to testify, but he wondered why he had to tell his story again when he already had done it in public a few years earlier.

Roselli, however, would not have to worry about rehashing old news. A week after dining with Trafficante, Roselli left his house to play golf; he never returned home. The police found his car at the municipal airport, but he had disappeared. On August 7, 1976, his body was found stuffed in an oil drum. He had been strangled and stabbed repeatedly, and his legs chopped off so he could fit into the oil drum.

Trafficante became a prime suspect in Roselli's murder when police heard a tape of a conversation between some Chicago mobsters. Trafficante had botched the disposal of Roselli's body, they gossiped. Later, the Tampa mobster was suspected of having something to do with the murder of Frank Bompensiero, a San Diego Mob leader and government informant who had reportedly told the FBI that he was involved in Roselli's murder. Bompensiero was shot to death in a phone booth on February 10, 1977.

Then on July 30, 1975, Jimmy Hoffa disappeared before the Church Committee could call him to testify. Hoffa was last seen sitting in the back seat of a car, leaning forward to talk to the driver. The FBI later discovered Hoffa's blood and hair in the car, but his body was never found. In 1983 Hoffa was declared legally dead. Ragano later told the press that Trafficante had told him he knew what happened to his old pal Jimmy Hoffa.

Meanwhile, the Church Committee hearings were becoming an eye opener for Americans. In late May 1975, CIA Director William Colby testified about his agency's involvement in assassination plots. Frank Church described Colby's testimony as "candid and chilling," explaining, "It is simply intolerable that an agency of the government of the United States may engage in murder." CIA witnesses told the Church Committee that the CIA had full authority to proceed against Castro, but U.S. government officials, especially those from the Kennedy era, claimed general ignorance of the assassination campaign, although they did acknowledge that there was an active anti-Castro campaign.

In October 1976, Trafficante made a secret four-hour appearance before the Church Committee to answer questions about his role in the CIA plots to kill Castro. The godfather was also questioned about whether the murders of John Roselli and Sam Giancana were connected to the fact they were to appear before the Church Committee. Most Church Committee members refused to comment, but committee member Robert T. Stafford acknowledged that Trafficante had, in fact, appeared before the committee.

By the time the Church Committee completed its work, it had done perhaps the most extensive review of American intelligence activities ever done by Congress. In 1975 and 1976, it published 14 reports that covered the history of the U.S. intelligence agencies and operations, the alleged abuses of power and the proposed recommendations for change. The Committee "condemned the assassination and rejects it as an instrument of American policy." Noting that the U.S. had no statute making it a crime to assassinate a foreign leader, it recommended "the prompt enactment of a statute making it a federal crime to commit or attempt assassination, or conspire to do so."

Even prior to Trafficante being called to testify before the Church Committee, the U.S. Senate was already talking about taking a new look into the JFK assassination. In April 1975, Virginia congressman Thomas Downing introduced a resolution calling on Congress to reopen the JFK assassination. Some startling revelations helped spur the move for an investigation. Jack Ruby, Oswald's killer, had also been a FBI informant, a fact brought to light only after a 1964 letter to FBI Director J. Edgar Hoover was obtained under the Freedom of Information Act. It was also discovered that several key witnesses had changed their testimony under pressure from the FBI.

Then in July 1976, the press revealed that FBI agent James Hostig had destroyed the letter Oswald had delivered to the FBI office in Dallas warning him to leave his family alone. Questions of a cover up were raised; more than 100 congressmen said they would back a resolution to establish a committee to investigate the Kennedy assassination. But the resolution failed to get out of committee, killed by a tie vote.

Still, the clamor on Capitol Hill for an investigation got louder. In September 1975, Senator Richard S. Schweiker (R-PA) told U.S. News and World Report that he was backing a review of the Kennedy case because "newly uncovered evidence has raised serious questions." Schweiker said that the CIA and FBI had covered up evidence that would have affected the Warren Commission conclusion that Lee Harvey Oswald had acted alone.

"Up until a few weeks ago, I was one who believed the Warren Commission's conclusion that Oswald had acted alone," Schweitzer explained. "But all these new developments have caused me to question some of the Commission's assumptions. I think there are certain grounds for taking another look. To me, it's like a big public ball that's going to burst."

A group of congressmen began working to form a select committee to investigate the deaths of both John Kennedy and Martin Luther King, Jr. Their efforts led to Resolution 1540, introduced on September 14, 1976, and passed by a vote of 280 to 65 on September 30. After the U.S.

Congress created the U.S. Senate Committee on Assassinations in 1976, it took another two years before the committee finally held hearings

The Committee granted Trafficante immunity from prosecution if he testified, but it threatened him with contempt if he refused. Trafficante testified on September 28, 1978. Earlier in the day, Lewis McWillie made his dramatic appearance at the hearing. He told the committee that Ruby had once spent a maximum of six days visiting him in Cuba. "I know for a fact he wasn't there over six days when he visited me," McWillie deadpanned "I couldn't have stood it any longer. Jack Ruby was the kind of fellow that six days would have been enough to be around him." The committee produced Cuban government documents to show when Ruby arrived and left Cuba, but it was noted that U.S. bank records contradicted this "evidence."

Jose Aleman, the Trafficante associate who had claimed to have been in a meeting with Trafficante in which he had predicted Kennedy would be "hit", also testified. He had no doubt Trafficante had direct links to the Cuban government, said Aleman. A committee memorandum had summarized a previous interview the committee had with Aleman in 1977. "Aleman confirms reports that S.T. (Santo Trafficante), made clear to him (implicitly) that he was not queasy about the killing (JFK); rather, he was giving the impression that he knew Kennedy was going to be killed. Aleman did not believe S.T. was personally involved in whatever plan he seemed to know about."

Now before Congress, Aleman changed his story, claiming he was not familiar with the term "hit" and that he thought Trafficante meant the voters would defeat Kennedy. If he believed Trafficante was talking about doing harm to the President, Aleman assured the committee, "I would have immediately advised the proper authorities." The witness was obviously frightened. Earlier, he had expressed concerns that Trafficante or Cuba or both were planning to do him harm, and he complained that the U.S. government had not provided him with a security detail when he arrived in Washington from Miami to testify. Given his "dramatic change in testimony," the committee allowed him to leave the hearing room.

When it came to Trafficante's turn to testify, he described himself as being retired and living in North Miami; however, he acknowledged publicly for the first time that he participated in the CIA's anti-Castro campaign, explaining his reason: "It was World War II. They tell you to go to the draft board and sign up. Well, I signed up."

The godfather elaborated, sounding much like an American patriot. "At the time I thought it was a good thing because Castro established a communist base 90 miles from the United States and because the United States wanted it done." He claimed his only role in the plot was to act as an interpreter between the English speaking CIA agents and the Spanish speaking anti-Castro Cuban exiles.

He denied knowing Ruby, and he scoffed at the notion that he knew Kennedy would be killed. "I'm sure I didn't; I'm positive I didn't," Trafficante said. "There was no reason to say that."

He did talk with Aleman in Miami in 1965, Trafficante conceded, about a possible Teamster's Union loan, but he recalled that the two talked in Spanish because the others in the room did not know English well.

On the final day of the hearings organized crime expert Ralph Salerno, an investigator with the New York Police Department, put Trafficante's testimony in perspective for the Committee, telling its members that it would be "naïve" to accept Trafficante's testimony at face value." Salerno found it inconceivable that a leading mobster like Trafficante would act in a Mob contract in such a minor role.

"There is no way Trafficante would have acted as an interpreter for the Cuban conspirators, or his fellow mobsters, Roselli and Giancana, considering his high rank as Mafia boss for Southern Florida," Salerno explained.

As for Jack Ruby's connection with the Mafia, Salerno said it was possible but unlikely that the Mafia would have used Ruby to do anything important for them, although sometimes it did use undependable people. "Jack Ruby would not have made a pimple on organized crime figure's back," Salerno testified. "But my professional opinion is that there is no evidence that the National Commission or La Cosa Nostra directed or approved the assassination of President Kennedy." The hearings lasted 17 days, the last three of which were made public. As the Committee wound up the public hearings on the John F. Kennedy phase of its investigation, the Committee's counsel told its members that organized crime's involvement in JFK's murder was still an open question. Nothing that has been uncovered contradicts it, and much that is new points to it and the means to do the assassination," said Committee counsel G. Robert Blakey. According to Blakey, organized crime had the motive, the opportunity and the means to do the assassination. But in his closing remarks, the Committee chairman Louis B. Stokes cautioned the public about making too much of conspiracy theories. "The Committee may find, as the Warren Commission did, but for different reasons, that Kennedy died at the hands of a lone assassin."

In all, 350 witnesses appeared before the Committee on the Kennedy assassination inquiry and well over 300 exhibits were put on the record. Investigators made 385 trips to 564 places to talk to 1548 people. More than 500 files from government agencies were reviewed, including the FBI file on Lee Harvey Oswald., which alone consisted of 238 volumes.

The Committee had to take this massive documentation and boil it down into a final report, a feat completed in less than three months. Still, many were not impressed. One Kennedy Aassassination expert described the Kennedy assassination hearings as "studied superficiality." "I don't believe these public sessions have ever been reflective of the total investigation," explained Robert Katz, Director of the Assassination Information Bureau. "The total investigation exists on two levels and what they have done so far is to make points they consider politically appropriate."

There was not anything "politically appropriate" about the Church Committee's final report, though, which became public on July 16, 1979. The politically correct conclusion to draw would have been to lay to rest the suspicion that a major conspiracy was responsible for JFK's assassination. Instead, the Committee added fuel to one of the major conspiracy theories about how JFK was assassinated.

The Committee concluded that, even though Oswald probably killed President Kennedy in Dallas, Texas, on November 23, 1963, "it is possible… that an individual organized crime leader or small combination of leaders might have participated in a conspiracy." Moreover, they had "the motive, means and opportunity" to assassinate President Kennedy." The report named Trafficante and fellow mobster Carlos Marcello as "the most likely family bosses of organized crime to have participated in such a unilateral assassination plot."

7
HEATING UP

THE INVESTIGATION OF the 20th century's most shocking assassination put Trafficante under intense public scrutiny, but he continued to be a power on the national Mob scene. That was evident in his suspected involvement in the hit of another powerful crime boss, Carmine Galante. In 1974 the violent and thuggish Galante took over the reins of the Bonanno crime family, replacing Joe Bonanno who had instigated a Mafia war in the 1960s after suspecting other crime family leaders were conspiring to kill him. Galante, who was known as "The Cigar" because he always had one dangling from his mouth, was tough and fearless, but his fellow crime bosses from the five ruling Mafia families detested him as a godfather with whom it was tough to get along. The bad news-- Galante turned out to be just as divisive a mobster as Joe Bonanno.

Galante was involved in a heroin network that became known as the Pizza Connection and included native Sicilian Mafioso as well as Sicilian immigrants to the U.S. The Pizza Connection began in 1975 and eventually mushroomed into a $1.65 billion drug smuggling operation that imported heroin from the Middle East and cocaine from South America and distributed the drugs through U.S. pizzeria storefronts, hence the name of the connection. The ring was smashed in 1984 when Italian authorities arrested a number of key drug traffickers at the Palermo airport trying to smuggle huge amounts of cash into the country.

Carmen Galante was involved in the Pizza Connection case, and law enforcement authorities suspect that, for whatever reason, he paid the ultimate price for it. On July 12, 1979, Galante was shot to death while eating lunch at Joe and Mary's Italian Restaurant in New York City. The cigar never fell from his mouth. It is believed the hit on Galante was the result of a unanimous decision of the Mafia's National Commission and that as a powerful player on the international drug scene, Trafficante was involved.

His ties with the drug trade remained strong, even after the French Connection was broken up in the early 1970s. In the mid 1970s, Trafficante made several trips to Central and South America where the authorities believe he brokered many heroin and cocaine deals with Latin American drug gangs. Tampa Mob historian Scott Deitche gives this assessment of Trafficante's relationship to the Latin American drug trade: "The deals he made with those factions enabled Trafficante to make some money from the trade without getting directly involved." Deitche concluded: "Trafficante may arguably be partially responsible for the flood of cocaine and the rise of Latin American drug gangs in this country."

His assessment is not an over statement. In the late 1970s, Colombian drug traffickers working for such gangs as the Medellin Cartel and the Cali Cartel were helping to make cocaine the major drug problem in the U.S. Trafficante was, no doubt, an important broker in the distribution pipeline that fueled the growth of the international cocaine connection. While Trafficante's name was nowhere to be found in the Pizza Connection indictment that came down in 1984, it did appear on a money laundering chart that outlined the movement of money by Sicilian crime bosses through offshore accounts to Filippo Salamone and other members of his crime family.

The Pizza Connection showed how difficult it was to tie Trafficante to a criminal operation. By the end of the 1970s, the authorities had a lot of suspicions, connections and accumulated details, but Trafficante was still walking the streets, a free man. Law enforcement has faced few mobsters as formidable as Trafficante. He was not only ruthless but brilliant, and he ran a tight ship.

Trafficante's gambling operations were a big part of his illicit business empire, and the FBI had been trying to infiltrate them for some time. The Bureau decided to take the initiative and it set up a gambling club at King's Court in the Florida town of Holiday, which is about an hour northeast of Tampa. It equipped King's Court with a surveillance system that included sound and video recording devices. Memberships were $25 and members were allowed to bring their own liquor so that the club wouldn't have to worry about getting a liquor license.

King's Court, however, was not attracting the kind of clientele the FBI hoped to catch. So it brought in Joseph Pistone, an ace undercover operative who used the name Donnie Brasco when he infiltrated the Bonanno crime family in New York City. Pistone's work as an undercover cop would later be the basis of the movie Donnie Brasco, which starred Johnny Depp as Brasco and Al Pacino as Benjamin "Lefty" Ruggiero, Brasco's closest contact in the Bonanno crime family.

Brasco told Dominick "Sonny Black" Napolitano, a high-ranking mobster in the Bonanno crime family, about the King's Court club, and he began to make regular visits to Holiday City with Brasco. King's Court was Santo Trafficante's territory, so Napolitano followed Mafia protocol and arranged a courtesy visit with the godfather. Trafficante agreed to allow the Bonanno family to expand their operations locally.

To ensure that the local police would not interfere, the Mob reportedly recruited Captain Joseph Donahue of the Pasco Sheriff's Department, who agreed to protect King's Court in return for a small payoff fee that amounted to a mere $2,500 for the period from November 1979 to January 1981.

Another mobster named Vincent "Jimmy" Aquafreda, who had a connection to the Lucchese crime family, also got caught in the sting. Aquafreda was working on a scheme that would have given him a monopoly over garbage collection on Florida's West Coast. The undercover operation at King's Court became known as Coldwater, a loose translation of the Spanish word "Aquafreda's."

The FBI monitored Napolitano's movements when he came to Florida, hoping they would finally get on tape some incriminating evidence that they could use against Trafficante. In June 1980, Napolitano finally met with Trafficante at Pappas, a popular restaurant in the city of Tarpon Springs. Also at the meeting was Vincent LoScalzo, a young mobster who Trafficante was grooming as his replacement.

The meeting went so well that Napolitano loosened up and blabbed about Trafficante on the tape: "There is so much money in Florida that if the old man dies, I'll move right down here and take over the whole state," Napolitano boasted.

Trafficante and Napolitano met several times over the next couple of months, but they did not meet in a setting that the FBI could bug. The Feds did manage to bug one of their meetings at the Tahitian Motor Lodge on U.S. Highway 19, close to King's Court, but when Trafficante entered the room, he turned up the volume on the TV, effectively neutralizing the bug. Another meeting on June 17, 1981, failed to produce any evidence either.

Sheriff's deputies finally raided King's Court on Las Vegas Night, a special gambling night that attracted many high rollers and a lot of money. The police hauled away $20,000 in cash, as well as guns, slot machines and other evidence. It would be the closest the authorities would get to Trafficante and the Tampa Mob scene. The FBI pulled Donnie Brasco off the case after war broke out between rival factions of the Bonanno family and shut down Operation Coldwater.

The FBI indicted Trafficante and eleven other men implicated in Operation Coldwater, including Napolitano, Aquafreda and Donahue. As the case was about to go to trial, Donahue killed himself in his home. Napolitano had let

Brasco into the Bonanno family and for that transgression he would have to pay. Napolitano's body was found in a drainage ditch. Meanwhile, most of the Bonanno family members on trial were found guilty.

Health wise, Trafficante was not doing well, and the case must have taken a toll on him. The old godfather looked frail in his final appearance in court. He was known to have heart trouble, his kidneys were failing, and later it was learned that Trafficante also had skin cancer. He was also losing sight in his left eye and the hearing in his left ear.

Since Trafficante was in poor health, his lawyers were able to get the trial postponed several times. Just when the trial was finally about to begin, the judge acquitted Trafficante, citing a lack of evidence. The decision stunned the Feds. They had missed their best chance to put the godfather behind bars.

Trafficante's legal problems, though, were not over. On June 4, 1981, a Federal grand jury indicted him and fifteen others in connection with kickbacks involving the Laborer's International Union of North America. The indictment accused the defendants of "conspiring to violate the Racketeering Influenced and Corrupt Organization (RICO) statute by giving and receiving unlawful kickbacks and for generating illegal union business involving the pension fund, life insurance and medical and dental plans." The press noted that Trafficante had never before been indicted for a major crime. As we have seen, the Donnie Brasco sting was still to come.

Trafficante was indicted with Raymond L.S. Patriarca, reputedly the Mob boss from Providence, Rhode Island. Atlee W. Wampler III, the U.S. Attorney in Miami, informed the press that Patriarca had told a government witness in 1976 that the Laborer's Union insurance business "would be controlled by 'the family.'" Patriarca allegedly told the government witness that the insurance business would be divided into territories, with Patriarca controlling the union's northeast insurance business, Anthony (Joe Batters) Accardo of Chicago controlling the Midwest and Santo Trafficante the South.

The trial began in Miami about a year later on April 12, 1982. The U.S. Justice Department lawyers and federal investigators were on the record stating that the case was one of the most important of recent racketeering prosecutions. They said the trial would establish that organized crime controlled the Laborer's International Union, which represented 30,000 skilled and unskilled laborers in the construction industry.

After a two-week trial, the jury reached its verdict. Six of the eight defendants were convicted, but two of the big fish, Anthony Accardo and Terrance J. O'Sullivan, the union's former secretary treasurer and later head of the Worldwide Insurance Company, were acquitted. The jury could not reach a verdict against the remaining defendants. The government still needed to try five more of the indicted, including Santo Trafficante, whom the press, when reporting on the case, was describing as "one of the last of the old-time Mafia dons" and the "head of one of the 26 organized crime families in the country."

While Trafficante still had the reputation of being a powerful godfather, his health problems continued to worsen, and he began to fade slowly from the Mob scene that he had dominated for more than thirty years. Trafficante had changed the course of history, but now hounded by the government, the godfather had to spend much of his time trying to stay out of jail. He was scheduled to go on trial in Miami in the case of the corrupt Laborer's International Union, but he got a temporary postponement at the last minute after he was admitted to the Tampa General Hospital because of an abdominal infection.

Trafficante had more than the Laborer's International Union corruption trial to worry about. The FBI was also investigating whether he was involved in still another corruption scandal. Allegations were made that Trafficante had met with a Miami lawyer to discuss making a $10,000 payoff to the lawyer to get U.S. District Judge Alcee Hastings to drop racketeering charges in the Laborer's International Union case. The FBI reported seeing monthly meetings between Hastings, the lawyer and Trafficante in Miami and Washington, although the bureau did concede its agents did not see any money change hands.

Tampa citizens knew little about Trafficante's current health situation, but a major feature article in the April 1982 issue of Tampa Magazine put his life in perspective for local residents. "The godfather's skin is drooping into pouches, his once robust-complexion turning sallow," wrote author Edward P. Whelan. "The confident gait is slower now, and he is rapidly losing weight. The gaunt old man remains cloistered in Tampa at the Parkland Estates home of his daughter and her husband, recuperating from a delicate kidney operation he endured this winter at Lakeland General Hospital…. His sight is failing and his hearing fades…."

The article probed Trafficante's alleged criminal ties, while providing a portrait of him as a loving family man. "He's concerned about everyone," Santos son-in-law Augie Paniello told Whelan. "He tells his grandson, Santo, named after him, that if he wants to make something of himself in life, he must work hard in college. He is very philosophical. I could not ask for a better father-in-law."

Even a FBI source seemed respectful. "His input may not be what it once was because of his health," the source told Whalen, "but his name still carries as much respect as any Mafia boss in the country."

The Federal government continued to keep the heat on the old godfather. In December 1982, Federal authorities filed a racketeering indictment that touched the Trafficante crime family. In what became known as Operation Super Bowl, they arrested 69 individuals, including Santo Trafficante III, the godfather's grandson, on charges of gambling. The jury found Lou Caggiano, one of the ring leaders, guilty and sentenced him to five years in prison, but in a move that had been repeated many times, the jury found Trafficante, Jr. innocent.

During the trial, the godfather's name came up not in relation to gambling but to another event far away from Tampa. It was a graphic example of his global reach. Rafael Trujillo, the dictator of Dominican Republic had allegedly approached Jack Sullivan, an associate of Meyer Lansky, with an offer to assassinate the president of Venezuela. Sullivan then reportedly subcontracted the contract to Santo Trafficante Jr., who, in turn, approached Johnny Rivera about doing the hit. It is believed Rivera actually journeyed to Venezuela to do the job, but the contract was cancelled when someone else killed the Venezuelan President first.

As these events unfolded, Trafficante was spending more time in hospitals than he was running his crime business. In March 1987, the Godfather was admitted to a Houston, Texas hospital to undergo a triple bypass operation. The doctors battled to save his life, but he did not survive. Santo Trafficante, Jr. died on March 17 at 8:17 a.m.

Three days later, family members and friends attended a 30-minute service at the C.E. Prevatt Funeral Home in Temple Terrace, Tampa. Across the street, a law enforcement officer sat in a late model car parked by a tree, taking photographs. Trafficante was taken to L'Unione Italiana Cemetery, where many of its granite markers are in Italian as well as English. About a 100 people, some of them dabbing their eyes, watched as Trafficante's casket was carried by eight pallbearers and placed in a small open area within a mausoleum.

FBI and local law enforcement officers were there as well, some of them taking photographs of the ceremony from what they considered to be a discrete distance. Their visible presence, though, angered many of the mourners. "Vulture bastards," one of the mourners reportedly said.

None of the country's major Mob figures attended the funeral, but Frank Ragano, Trafficante's long-time lawyer, came to pay his respects. He told the press: "I lost a friend. It's a shame we don't have more like him. He was a man of his word. A handshake was his bond." Then Ragano waxed philosophical: "A lot of people judged him on earth, but the final judge will be God."

But men on earth were already judging the Trafficante legacy. Webster Jackson, 58-year old man who watched the service from across the street, marveled: "It's almost incredible, isn't it? You and I do the least little thing, and we spend several days (in jail). Whatever his world was, he had to be great in it."

The St. Petersburg Times interviewed Ralph Salerno by the phone from his winter home in Naples, Florida. Salerno was the organized crime expert who nearly a decade before had testified about Trafficante at the congressional hearings on the JFK assassination. Salerno described Trafficante's death as the "end of an era" because "he's really the last of the old-time leaders. He's one of the few remnants of the old leadership that held those positions."

Other law enforcement officials wondered abut the information Trafficante took to his grave. "I would have liked to have had the opportunity to interview him in depth prior to the time he died," Bill James, a Florida state attorney, told the St. Petersburg Times. "I think he could have given some interesting information."

The opportunity would never come. Trafficante never revealed what he knew about the

CIA, JFK, Hoffa, Roselli, Giancana, Galante, the international drug trade and the seminal events of the late 20th century to which he may have been connected. In death, he would remain as enigmatic, mysterious and controversial as he was in running his criminal empire.

8
EPILOGUE

SANTO TRAFFICANTE, JR. dominated the Tampa Mafia scene for more than three decades, so it was unclear if, after his death, the transition to a new era would go smoothly. As Tampa Mafia historian Scott Deitche explained: "The Trafficante family was still making money, but in terms of leadership, its future was uncertain. There were several crime organizations in Tampa, each with their own leaders and agendas."

The authorities did not really know if Trafficante had chosen someone to be his successor, although they did had some candidates: Fano and Henry Trafficante, Santo's brothers; Frank Diecidue, a 72-year old Tampa businessman and under boss in the crime family; and Frank Albano, a restaurant owner who was married to a niece of Santo's and also worked in sales for a vending company; and Vincent Salvatore LoScalzo, Trafficante's former bodyguard.

In reality, Henry Trafficante was not a prime candidate because he did not get along with Santo, Jr. He ran a gambling ring in the early 1950s that brought unwanted attention to the crime family. The police raided Henry's gambling establishments, much to displeasure of Santo, Jr. "Henry was rarely seen in the surveillance of Santo," Deitche writes. "When they were together, many witnesses saw visible signs of tension."

Fano, a bar owner, had better relations with Santo Jr., but he died in 1991 at age 72. Frank Diecidue had a long and close relationship with Santo. The FBI had identified Diecidue as a Trafficante underboss in 1957, the year he went to the landmark Apalachin meeting. In 1976, he was charged with racketeering in an indictment that implicated others with participating in a plot to kill Tampa police detective Richard Cloud. Diecidue was convicted of the charge and spent time in federal prison before an appeals court overturned his conviction.

LoScalzo was probably the best candidate. Rumors had circulated from the late 1970s that the aging godfather had been grooming LoScalzo as his successor. LoScalzo was born in 1937 in Allesandria Della Rocca, the same town from which the Trafficantes emigrated, and he followed the Trafficante family tradition by keeping in close contact with the Marcello crime family. LoScalzo had never been charged with a crime, although the authorities forced him to give up a liquor license, and two years before Santo's death, they had sought an injunction to close a bar he owned named Ernesto's Bar and Package Store.

Could LoScalzo be Trafficante's choice? An interesting event that happened at the Italian Club in Ybor City, the day before the funeral, made many people think so. According to Deitche, "It's alleged that over seventy low-level associates of the crime family filed past LoScalzo, kissing his ring and paying their respects."

But whether LoScalzo actually became Tampa's boss of bosses was thrown in question four years later by a 1991 St. Petersburg Times' newspaper report. In looking at court records and testimony, the newspaper concluded that LoScalzo was actually sharing the leadership with Frank Diecidue and Frank Albano.

As the Trafficante crime family adjusted to life without Santo, Jr., a controversial period in Mafia history was also coming to a close in Louisiana. On March 2, 1993, Carlo Marcello, Trafficante's close friend and the last remaining player from the days of the CIA's "Kill Castro" campaign, died in his sleep at age 83 at his Metairie home. The cause of Marcello's death was unknown, but it was believed that Marcello had Alzheimer's disease. He was in failing health for several years and had lived in seclusion since his

1989 release from federal prison. It was his fourth term behind bars in his lifetime battle with law enforcement.

Marcello was not as adept at evading the law as Trafficante had been. In 1981 Marcello and Charles Roemer, the former Louisiana Commissioner of Administration, were convicted of conspiring to obtain kickbacks from the state's insurance business. In the same year, a court convicted Marcello of conspiring to bribe a Federal judge who was about to proceed with a Mob trial in California.

Many people believed—and still do—that Marcello, like Trafficante, had escaped justice for conspiracy to kill President John F. Kennedy. Both Trafficante and Marcello, however, adamantly denied any involvement to their graves. Robert Goldfarb worked for Robert Kennedy in the Justice Department organized crime section from 1961 to 1964. In a March 13, 1993 article in The Washington Post, Goldfarb noted: "Though there is reasonable suspicion that the long-time Mafia boss helped mastermind the JFK assassination, he has finally eluded the persistent investigations. His file, should not however, close the file on the Mob and the JFK murder."

On the face of it, such a conspiracy does not seem plausible. After all, the National Ruling Crime Commission of the Italian American Mafia would need to approve such a mega hit.

But would a normally cautious Mafia Commission really do that and risk having the full fury of the American judicial system come down on it?

In 1991 film director Oliver Stone released his movie, JFK, rekindling interest in the conspiracy theory. Stone is an acclaimed director who has won best director Oscars for Platoon (1986) and Born on the Fourth of July (1989) and another Oscar for best screenplay adaptation for Midnight Express (1978). The movie JFK championed the assassination probe of New Orleans District Attorney Jim Garrison, who in 1967 speculated that Oswald had defected to the Soviet Union, sought asylum in Cuba and had shady connections to the anti-Castro Cuban militant exile community. In focusing on Garrison as the movie's hero, Stone accused the FBI, CIA, Cuban exiles, U.S. military intelligence and former president Lyndon Baines Johnson of all playing a role in the assassination.

Stone said the purpose of his movie was to "interpret history in order to create lasting universal truths. Our film's mythology—hopefully—will replace the Warren Report, as Gone with the Wind replaced Uncle Tom's Cabin, which, in turn, was replaced by Roots. Critics blasted Stone's movie for what they said was mixing fact with fiction and making a confusing movie about one of the most confusing events of the 20th century. But the movie did have an impact. It is credited with helping to push Congress to pass the Assassinations Materials Disclosure Act of 1994, which has since led to the release of more records relating to JFK's assassination.

The following year, Frank Ragano, the lawyer who had represented Trafficante and other organized crime figures for more than thirty years, dropped a bombshell. I carried a message from Teamster's boss Jimmy Hoffa to Trafficante and Marcello: Kill the President, Ragano told the press. He expected the two godfathers to laugh when they heard the message, but they didn't. "They glanced at each other in a very serious vein."

Critics jumped on Ragano accusing him of being a huckster who was trying to generate publicity for his forthcoming autobiography. A 1990 conviction on charges of tax invasion did get him suspended from practicing law, and he may have needed money. But G. Robert Blakey, the chief counsel of the House Assassinations Committee, told the St. Petersburg Times that Ragano's story was "most plausible."

The year 1993 marked the 30th anniversary of JFK's assassination. No subject in modern American history has so fascinated the American public, and in the three decades since 1993, more than 2000 books had been written about the subject, representing a wide assortment of perspectives.

More books were published in the anniversary year. One of the most controversial was indirectly related to the John Kennedy assassination: a probing biography of Jimmy Hoffa, written by investigative journalist Dan Moldea and providing interesting information about a possible Mob connection to JFK's assassination. "There is no doubt in my mind that Hoffa, Trafficante and Marcello were all involved in the plot," Moldea told the Cleveland Plain Dealer. In reporting on Moldea's explosive book, the Plain Dealer noted, "Through his investigative books frequently have been lashed by critics questioning the accuracy and relevancy of his reporting, Moldea is being sought these days as an alternative source on national talk shows and television documentaries whenever the topic of the assassination of Hoffa has been discussed." Books touching on the JFK assassination do indeed sell.

In the same year, investigative journalist Gerald Posner caused an uproar when he published Case Closed: Lee Harvey Oswald and The Assassination of JFK, a book that supported the Warren Commission's conclusion that Oswald acted alone. The Warren Commission had properly investigated the JFK assassination, Posner concluded. JFK assassination conspiracy theorists considered Posner's book an outrage, and it was attacked for what they claimed where numerous errors and distortions. Some reviewers welcomed the book. Writing in The Saginaw News, Dr.

Grover B. Proctor Jr., an historian and expert on the JFK assassination, described Posner's book as "being thorough, clearly written, well-edited and exhaustively footnoted and indexed."

Posner's book, however, failed to lay to rest the idea that a conspiracy of some kind was responsible for Kennedy's death. For many Americans, too many questions remained unanswered, and speculation about the Mob's connection to the JFK assassination persisted. In 1993, G. Robert Blakey, the Chief Counsel to the House Assassinations Committee, co-authored a book titled Fatal Hour: the Assassination of President Kennedy that concluded Trafficante and Marcello were involved in the assassination.

In a 1993 interview on the PBS television show Frontline, Blakey said that the prosecution's case against Oswald is open and shut. "If he had shot his brother-in-law in the backseat of a convertible, and not the President of the United States, he (Oswald) would have been tried, convicted and forgotten in three days." Still, the case was not closed. For Blakey, "the crucial question in 1963 is the crucial question in 1993. It's not whether Oswald killed Kennedy? He did. It's whether he had help in any way."

Blakey revealed that the FBI had an illegal electronic surveillance program in place that focused on the major figures in organized crime nationwide, including Trafficante and the Tampa

Mafia. "We were looking for some evidence in these men's conversations that would connect them to the assassination—to either of Lee Harvey Oswald or Ruby," Investigators did not find a smoking gun, but as Blakey recalled: "On the other hand, what we did find, shockingly, is repeated conversations by these people that indicated the depth of their hatred of Kennedy and actual discussions saying: he ought to be killed, he ought to be whacked."

Oswald did have a connection to organized crime, Blakey revealed. Oswald's uncle Charles "Dutch" Murret, a bookie, was under the control of Carlos Marcello. "These were the type of people who were in the sphere of Lee Harvey Oswald's life as a child," Blakey said.

The "evidence," though, was all tenuously connected, and some law enforcement officials on the front lines of the war against the Mafia had their doubts. For instance, Chicago FBI agent William Roemer spent hours listening to the wiretaps of mobsters after the assassination, but he said there was no talk of conspiracy.

This, too, does not mean that Trafficante and his associates were not involved in a conspiracy. The Mob careers of Trafficante and Marcello showed them to be cautious men, but caution, of course, can be interpreted in two ways. They were cautious because they knew they were being wiretapped. So being involved in the conspiracy, they thought it wise to say nothing. Or they were cautious because they had no intention of killing Kennedy, knowing full well the risks involved.

The thirty-year anniversary of JFK's death came and went, but still the controversy surrounding the assassination of the century would not die down. More investigative books followed in the years ahead. In 1994, Charles Furati published ZR Rifle: The Plot to Kill Kennedy and Castro, one of the few books in English on the JFK assassination that gave the Castro regime's point of view. His investigation, Furati said, was "based on information supplied by the Cuban State Security Department." According to Castro's secret police, Santo Trafficante, Jr. was among those responsible for the assassination. Lyndon Johnson was one who believed that Castro had had enough of the assassination attempts on his life and finally struck back, finding a willing assassin in Oswald, a known communist sympathizer. It's known that Oswald admired Castro, often referring to him as "Uncle Fidel."

In the same year, the publication of Robert Groden's book, The Search for Lee Harvey Oswald, continued to keep the Mob conspiracy theory in the news. Groden, the staff photographic consultant for the House Select Committee on Assassinations, did a careful examination of the photos of Oswald taken immediately before he was shot in the Dallas police station. His conclusion-- photos suggest that Oswald recognized his killer, Jack Ruby.

The following year, journalists Raymond and Mary La Fontaine purported to provide more evidence proving Oswald had Mob connections. Their book, Oswald Talked: the New Evidence in the JFK Assassination, was based, in part, on an interview they conducted with John Franklin Elrod, who, as a prisoner, had occupied a jail cell near Oswald's in the Dallas police station on the fateful night of November 22, 1963. Elrod claimed that Oswald told him he had recently attended a meeting at which Jack Ruby was present.

In 2005 two authors claimed to have the last word on whether Trafficante and the Mafia conspired to kill Kennedy. Lamar Waldron and Thom Hartmann drew from seven years of research, thousands of recently declassified files and dozens of interviews to write Ultimate Sacrifice. Their investigation did present some remarkable new information and drew conclusions that were shocking, even given all the books written and films and documentaries made about the assassination.

The Kennedy administration had a secret unknown plan for a coup in Cuba, code-named AmWorld, Waldron and Hartmann contended, and it involved Santo Trafficante, Carlos Marcello and Johnny Roselli. According to the authors, the three mobsters learned of Uncle Sam's secret coup plan and then used parts of it to plan the JFK assassination. After the assassination, the mobsters used the secrecy surrounding the plan to prevent a government investigation. The authors claimed that, in addition to their successful "coup" in Dallas on November 22, 1963, Trafficante and his associates actually made two other assassination attempts: one in Chicago on November 2, 1963, and a second in Tampa on November 18.

With their accumulation of detail, use of new documentation and thorough presentation, Waldron and Hartmann attempted to close the case for good. But could Trafficante and his associates have had it in them to plan, pull off and get away with it? We may never know. Critics have attacked Waldron and Hartmann's book, claiming to find holes in their thesis. Still as time passes, it becomes increasingly difficult to prove a conspiracy conclusively even with the release of more records or the discovery of new "evidence."

But if Trafficante were alive today and he was tried in a court of law, would the evidence convict him? Some experts believe so. Ronald Goldfarb says the circumstantial evidence is credible, and prosecutors often use it to present and win their cases. Goldfarb writes: "One could conclude from the existing credible evidence that there was a criminal conspiracy to kill the president, even if the best evidence to date indicates Oswald acted as lone assassin, and there is inadequate evidence of a link between Oswald's act and such a conspiracy. Ragano's reports about Trafficante's and Marcello's and Hoffa's incriminating remarks, along with testimony about Hoffa threats, and the report of Marcello's warning, and Giancana's brother's reports of their conversions and his boasts, combined with the fact of the killing, and the clear motive, arguably constitute a case of conspiracy that a jury might believe." If Trafficante were alive today, convicting him of such a mind-boggling crime, no matter how strong the circumstantial evidence, would not be a sure thing. As his long and remarkable criminal career showed, the incomparable crime boss always found a way to evade justice.

ACKNOWLEDGEMENTS

The author would like to thank those who helped make this book possible: David Weeks and Larry and Stephanie Vezina for reviewing the manuscript and offering valuable suggestions on how to improve it. Thanks also to Charles Lutz for reviewing the manuscript and sharing his law enforcement expertise with this and my other projects. Carrie Volk, Patti Stafford and Ann Thomas of the Winthrop University Library for providing library research assistance and for helping with interlibrary loan. Dean Mark Y. Herring, Winthrop Library, for his support and encouragement over the years. Thanks also the National Archives and Records Center in Washington, DC, for making government documents available. I would like to give special thanks to my wife, Magdalena, for her encouragement and support over the years.

FURTHER READING

Dietche, Scott M., *Cigar City Mafia*, Barricade Books, Fort Lee, 2004

———. *The Silent Don: The Criminal Underworld of Santo Trafficante*, Barricade books, 2009

Furati, Claudia, *ZR Rifle: The Plot to Kill Kennedy and Castro*, Ocean Press, New York, 1994

Pistone, Joseph D., *Donnie Brasco: My Undercover Life in the Mafia*, Signet Books, New York, 1997

Waldron, Lamar and Thom Hartmann, *Ultimate Sacrifice: John and Robert Kennedy, the Plan for a Coup in Cuba and the Murder of JFK*, Carroll & Graf Publishers, New York, 2005

INDEX

ABOUT THE AUTHOR

Ron Chepesiuk (www.ronchepesiuk.com) is an award-winning freelance investigative journalist and documentary producer. He is a Fulbright scholar to Indonesia and Bangladesh and a consultant to the History Channel's Gangland documentary series. His true crime books include Drug Lords, Black Gangsters of Chicago and Gangsters of Harlem. His book, Gangsters of Miami, will be published in the fall of 2009 and his book, Sergeant Smack: The Lives and Time of Ike Atkinson, Kingpin, and his Band of Brothers, will be published as an e-book in 2010. Ron's books have won numerous awards, including the IPPY, Foreword Magazine and U.S.A Book News and the National Indie Excellence awards.

THE LEGENDARY LIVES AND TIMES OF
IKE ATKINSON, KINGPIN,
AND HIS BAND OF BROTHERS

Sergeant Smack chronicles the story of Leslie "Ike" Atkinson, one of U.S. history's most original gangsters, Under the cover of the Vietnam War and through the use of the U.S. military infrastructure, Atkinson masterminded an enterprising group of family members and former African American GIs that the DEA identified as one of history's ten top drug trafficking rings. According to law enforcement sources, 1,000 pounds is a conservative estimate for the heroin amount the ring transported annually from Bangkok, Thailand, to U.S. military bases during its period of operation from 1968 to 1975. That amount translates to about $400 million worth of illegal drug sales during that period.

Ike Atkinson is a charismatic former U.S. army master sergeant, career smuggler, card shark and doting family man whom law enforcement code-named Sergeant Smack. He was never known to carry a gun, and, today, many retired law enforcement officials who put him in jail, refer to him as a "gentleman." Sergeant Smack's criminal activities sparked the creation of a special DEA unit code named Centac 9, which conducted an intensive three-year investigation across three continents. Sergeant Smack was elusive, but the discovery of his palm print on a kilo of heroin finally took him down.

In 1987, Ike tried to revive his drug ring from Otisville Federal Penitentiary, but the Feds discovered the plot and set up a sting. The events that follow seem like the narrative for a Robert Ludlum novel. Atkinson is convicted and nine years are added to his sentence. Ike was released from prison in 2006 after serving 31-year jail sentence. Atkinson's story is controversial because his ring has been accused of smuggling heroin to the U.S. in the coffins and cadavers of dead American GIs. As this book shows, the accusation is completely false.

The recent movie, "American Gangster," which depicted the criminal career of Frank Lucas, distorted Atkinson's historical role in the international drug trade. Sergeant Smack exposes the lies about the Ike Atkinson-Frank Lucas relationship and documents how Ike, not Lucas, pioneered the Asian heroin connection.